HANDMADE
PAPER CREATIONS

HANDMADE PAPER CREATIONS

30+ projects you can make to decorate your home or to give as gifts

Amelia Saint George

NORTH LIGHT BOOKS

Cincinnati, Ohio

*For my inquisitive daughter Abigail.
Over the years we have had a lot of
fun with paper: making doll's houses
from shoe boxes, transforming the
bunk beds into castles with
cardboard, turning boxes into
rowing boats or doll's cots.
Now walls are covered with pop star
découpage and paper lamps sketched
with flowers. Abigail has created so
many things, which in turn have
inspired this book.*

First published in North America in 1996 by
North Light Books,
an imprint of F&W Publications, Inc.
1507 Dana Avenue, Cincinnati, OH 45207
1-800/289-0963

First published in 1996 by
HarperCollins Publishers, London

ISBN 0-89134-740-2

*Edited by Geraldine Christy
Designed by Town Group Consultancy Ltd
Photography by Jon Bouchier*

For HarperCollins
*Editorial Director: Cathy Gosling
Design Manager: Caroline Hill*

Set in Berthold Imago, Bodoni,
Garamond and Shelley Andante
Colour origination by Colourscan, Singapore
Produced by Lego Spa, Italy

ACKNOWLEDGEMENT
The origami Santa Claus decoration
on page 88 is modified from an
original design by Yoshihde
Momntani (Japan).

CONTENTS

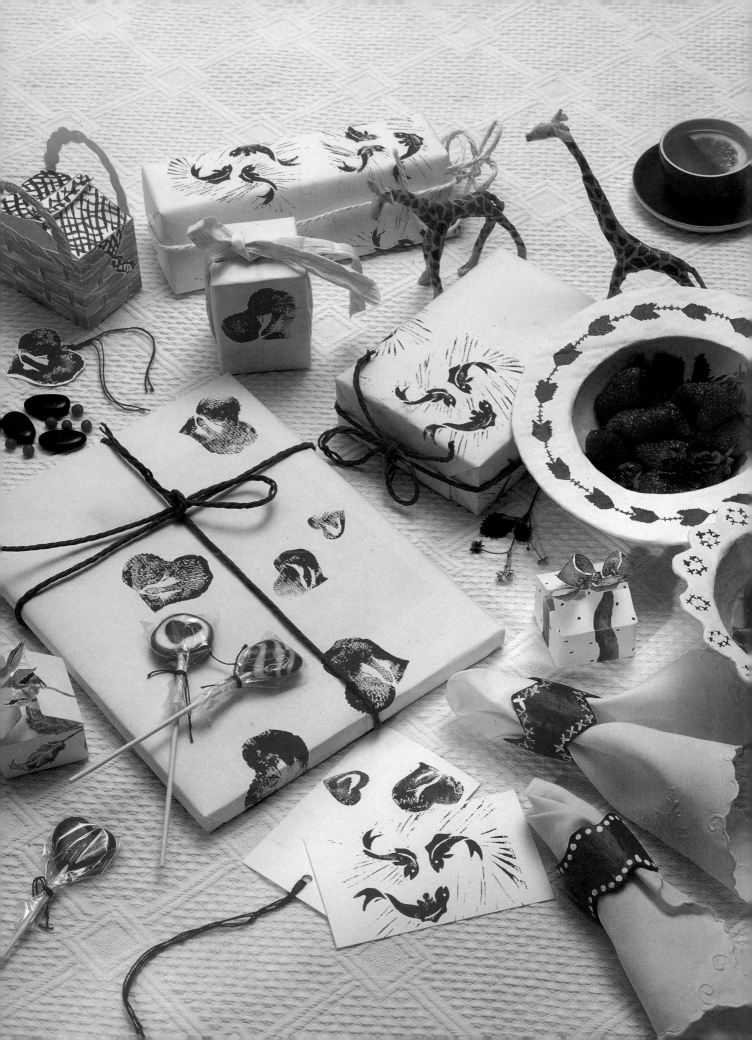

ꓕNTRODUCTION

Paper can be found everywhere and for every kind of use. This diverse and superb material surrounds us in infinite variety, from the newspapers we read each morning to hand-printed wall coverings.

Experimenting with paper is inexpensive and expressive. Its versatility in craftwork lends itself to any number of items, from light tissue-paper bowls to solid sculptured models made from papier mâché pulp. A seemingly ordinary-looking raw material, it can be transformed into a diversity of objects.

In writing this book I have rediscovered many of the crafts I enjoyed as a child – papier mâché, basket weaving and making booklets. However, a brief glance through the following pages at some of the projects will show you that these simple techniques can create elegant items similar to those for sale in sophisticated craft stores. Each chapter gives clear instructions to follow, with tricks to ensure success.

At the end of the book there are some design templates that you can cut out and use immediately, including four delightful boxes for trinkets or treasures, four decorated photograph frames and a charming small lampshade.

There are additional templates in the book that you can trace or photocopy to give swift and professional-looking results to your work. I have made all the items in the book myself, and have chosen them with the aim of providing you with a wide variety of differing skills. The ideas include covering a whole desk or decorating a small tray with découpage; using papier mâché to make shimmering gold-leaf bowls or a sculptured pig for the garden; printing with stencils, lino or stamps to enhance folders, wrapping paper and cards; cutting and slitting paper to decorate lampshades, or even a roller blind; pleating presents and making origami decorations for the Christmas tree. Younger children will enjoy creating an ark out of a cardboard box with all the animals, covering a frame with used stamps, or decorating their files to return to school.

The book gathers together many ideas, some new, some traditional, but makes the most of the wealth of modern materials available. Paper is easily acquired: please do have a go. I have thoroughly enjoyed making the projects in this book and I hope you do too.

A selection of plain coloured papers available for papercraft from art and craft suppliers. Many unique hand-made papers can also be obtained from specialist craft galleries.

$\mathscr{M}$ATERIALS AND EQUIPMENT

PAPERS

The range of papers that you can choose from is almost endless. There are exquisite marbled papers from Venice, delicate rice papers from Japan, trapped-fibre papers from India, papers incorporating wild flowers and corn husks from the USA, and gossamer-fine papers from France. Every hue possible can be found, from subtle neutral colours to the brightest of fluorescents, in numerous textures and in a variety of weights for use with watercolour, acrylic paint, pastel, crayon, pencil or pen.

The paper that you use will dictate the results of your work. Frequently you can cheat, use the wrong material and get away with it, but only experimentation can decide this for you. The most

Paper weights conversion table

150 gsm – 70 lb

190 gsm – 90 lb

300 gsm – 140 lb

400 gsm – 200 lb

535 gsm – 250 lb

GLUES

Throughout the book I have used mainly white PVA glue. Its advantage is that it can be watered down from a thick yoghurt-like consistency to a thin milky application. Always do a small test on a scrap piece of paper before using, however, especially when you are adding water, to judge if the paper is likely to buckle or become wrinkly when glue is applied.

The heavier the paper the more glue you can use. On very light papers I often use dry glue sticks, but they have a tendency to peel away after repeated use.

Repositionable spray glue is useful for temporary positioning, for instance when working with stencils, découpage and many other projects. Once you have a can in the cupboard you will wonder how you ever managed without it!

FIXATIVES AND VARNISHES

Both fixatives and varnishes are needed to protect your work. Use a light spray fixative to protect paper items such as lampshades or boxes (it certainly makes dusting easier). Apply varnishes to protect items that will have heavier use or need to be more durable, such as those decorated with découpage or for papier mâché objects. I mainly use acrylic water-soluble varnishes as

they are odourless, fast drying and do not yellow the work. However, a last coat of oil varnish will add durability to items used outside or that need extra protection. Always try the effects of varnishes on a scrap of paper before applying them to any item as they vary greatly.

CUTTING EQUIPMENT

Use a sharp craft knife or scalpel, with a cutting mat to protect surfaces, remembering always to cut away from you. A straightedge is also useful. Alternatively, you may prefer to use scissors; a sharp-pointed pair of embroidery scissors is convenient to handle and handy for cutting into corners.

If you are likely to cut a number of mounts from board it may be worth buying a mount cutter. There are a number of models suitable for craft use that will give a professional-looking finish.

PAINTS

For most of the projects in the book I have used acrylics as they dry quickly, are odourless, and water washable. Daler-Rowney have developed several ranges that I enjoy using. Rowney Cryla artists' acrylic colours are professional paints; they can be used as thickly as oils or thinned to the translucency of watercolour. Rowney Cryla Flow is a less expensive version of these colours; they do not have quite as much body, but give excellent results. Rowney System 3 acrylic paints have an easy, looser application. Once they are on my palette I use them for everything – over wood, on thicker papers and papier mâché, and for stencilling and wall painting. Test lighter papers before use.

important point to remember is that the weight of the paper you use should be appropriate to the item you are making. For instance, 150 and 190 gsm (70 and 90 lb) papers are both suitable weights for small boxes, lampshades or quality printing. For more robust use, such as files, booklets, or large lampshades and boxes, a heavier 535 gsm (250 lb) paper is recommended. For making mounts 1500 gsm (700 lb) is strong and unbendable.

COLOURS

I use only six primary colours:

Lemon Yellow – just the colour of a lemon, a yellow with a hint of blue.

Cadmium Yellow Pale – a stronger yellow with more red in it.

Cadmium Red – a strong basic red with a warm yellow hidden in it.

Crimson Alizarin – a deep red with a tendency towards blue.

Ultramarine – a wonderful deep blue with the warmth and depth of red within.

Coeruleum – a duller blue with a tendency to yellow.

If you place these colours in a circle you will have two yellows, two reds and two blues, giving you the ability to mix a range of colours with ease. By mixing colours related to each other you can achieve much clearer colours. For instance, Cadmium Red mixed with Cadmium Yellow gives a bright orange because both colours have a sympathy with one another – the Cadmium Red has yellow in it and the Cadmium Yellow has red in it . Thus they do not fight when mixed and produce a bright orange in all its force. Cadmium Red mixed with Lemon Yellow produces a duller orange because Lemon Yellow has a little blue in it, which fights against the yellow. Similarly, by adding blue to the bright orange the colours would fight and produce the duller

Add coloured decoration to your projects with watercolours, coloured pencils, acrylic paints, oil pastels or printing inks, using the appropriate brushes or roller. Basic specialized equipment includes a lino cutter and stencil brushes.

colour brown. Do experiment with mixing colours because it will be to your greatest benefit.

Two other colours I use are Payne's Grey, which is softer than black, and Titanium White, which has good body and mixes well.

PALETTES

In my opinion the best way to use acrylics is with a Stay-Wet Palette. Acrylics dry quickly but this palette keeps them wet from underneath. Even when my acrylics have been squeezed onto an open plate I keep a mist water-sprayer to hand, and cover the plate when not in use with film food wrap.

BRUSHES

Dalon artists' brushes are exceptionally versatile; I use mine for all applications from small detailed work to large papier mâché projects. A man-made imitation of sable, they are washable in water, occasionally in a light washing liquid, and bounce back after endless use. Brushes are important, so buy one or two good ones and look after them. Always use a reject brush for only glue.

SPECIALIZED PAINTS

Specialized paints are available for block printing; they are designed to be rolled out and used for linocuts.

Fabric acrylic-based paints can be bought for use on all natural fabrics. They are washable once fixed into the fabric by heat, either by ironing or, in the case of large pieces of material, by tumble dryer.

Oil pastels, coloured crayons and watercolours all give differing effects, depending on what you wish to achieve and how a particular papercraft item will be used.

Découpage is an attractive and cost-effective way of transforming many household objects by simply cutting out paper images and pasting them down onto whatever surface you choose. You can decorate a wide variety of items using découpage, from the smallest tray to a complete table, and create any number of unusual accessories to personalize your home. Many images are readily available in magazines, or on wrapping paper, and you can even use discarded photos or used stamps for découpage. An interesting effect is to link items thematically within a room, for instance by making a desk set to tone with a writing table or decorating a small box with stamps to match a mirror frame.

DÉCOUPAGE

Opposite *Découpage decoration used to transform an outdoor table setting.*

STEP BY STEP
*D*ECOUPAGE DISH

Fresh fruits and vegetables are a welcome sight throughout the year, and look attractive on table tops, trays or as decoration for the inside of the larder door. These charming images are effective in black and white, but give plenty of scope for artistic expression when you colour them in. Use either nature's colours or play with the images to create surprises such as orange, yellow and violet berries.

1 Photocopy some images from magazines, enlarging or reducing them to your own requirements; I have drawn some radishes. Colour the vegetables with paints or coloured pencils, using slightly deeper colour for the more shaded parts of the designs and little colour or wash for the lighter parts.

Materials
•
Dish or bowl
•
Exterior PVA glue
•
Brushes for paints and glue
•
Cutting knife and mat
•
Paints or coloured pencils
•
Acrylic varnish
•
Oil varnish

2 Cut out the vegetables with a cutting blade on a cutting mat, or use embroidery scissors. If you want to alter your images, do so; for instance if you require a radish with only two leaves, cut the extra ones off.

3 Glue down the radish onto the dish. As this image is quite delicate it is easier to lay the radish face down on the cutting mat and apply glue liberally over it. Then peel the radish off the cutting mat and lower it onto the dish, smoothing out the leaves gently with the brush. Wipe the glue off the cutting mat before it dries.

4 When the radish is dry apply a thick layer of white PVA glue over the top. The glue will dry to a transparent finish; it acts as a sealant and will prevent any varnish being absorbed by the paper and discolouring. Finally, when the glue is completely dry and clear, apply four coats of varnish to protect the découpage. Finish with a layer of oil varnish as a safeguard.

5 The finished dish makes an attractive addition to a garden meal. Protected by varnish, it can be used for salad vegetables, breads or fruit.

GARDEN TABLE

The metal garden table pictured on page 12 is a fairly common piece of garden furniture. Personalized with découpage it becomes an attractive talking point, and a fun addition to your garden. If the surface you are to découpage is unlikely to get very wet, your choice of glues and varnishes may not be too critical. This metal table stays outside in the English damp, drizzle and snow, however, so I used a water-resistant PVA glue, and then a clear, satin-finish, white spirit soluble varnish to seal the work. Also, I must admit that I slightly tilt the table when it is not in use so that the rain drains off.

Above *Overlap images for a natural effect. Here, slender shallots contrast well with a more solid corncob.*

Top right *Vegetable images are suitable découpage motifs for other outdoor items such as trays and watering cans.*

Découpage on metal

When applying découpage to items that are to be exposed to the elements it is important to choose an appropriate glue and varnish, otherwise your handiwork may be easily spoiled. If in doubt seek advice from your local supplier.

PLANNING THE DESIGN

First prepare the surface by rubbing down any rust and making sure that the table is clean and dry. Cut out the vegetables you have drawn or photocopied and plan their positions before gluing them down. Spread your images out over the area you are working on until you like the arrangement. I placed mine swirling around the edge of the table, combining large cabbages with delicate trailing radishes, and jostling maize with mushrooms.

Once you are happy with your arrangement, paint the back of each image with water-resistant exterior PVA glue and stick it into position. When placing the very fine shallot cut-outs, which tend to curl when painted with glue, I simply painted the glue onto the table, then smoothed the shallots onto it. Do not worry about glue spilling on the exposed metal, as it will become transparent when dry.

COLOURING THE IMAGES

When the glue has dried you can paint the images. I used acrylics, but as the varnish will protect your work you can use coloured pencils, gouache or watercolour if you prefer. You will find that photocopied images are toned with highlights and shadows so you need only apply a fairly thin even coat of paint in the colour of your choice. I painted some of the swedes in cream, and others in purple so that they would appear as beetroot.

PROTECTING THE SURFACE

Before varnishing, wait for the paint to dry, then glue down any images that are not firmly fixed. Dust the surface carefully. Then apply a clear, satin-finish varnish, one that is soluble in white spirit. You cannot sand découpage work between coats because you would damage the images. Instead, wipe gently with a lint-free rag slightly dampened with white spirit to remove any dust that might have fallen on your drying work. Allow each layer to dry thoroughly and then apply another coat until the images are fully covered. You will need to apply approximately ten coats.

Small boxes were covered in the same paper as this writing desk to provide extra storage. Red luggage labels tone with the boxes and identify their contents clearly.

𝒲RITING TABLE

This practical little table had seen better days and I decided to cover it. I found an old hand-written deed for a house and colour-photocopied it, including its seals and ribbons. Photocopying allows you to arrange the colour tones as you wish, perhaps a little more yellow and a muted red to suggest antiquity, and you can adapt the scale of the design. I had the writing enlarged slightly for the table, which I felt suited its proportions better. When covering the boxes, which were smaller, I used the original size.

MEASURING UP

I calculated how much paper I would need by first covering the table with A4 sheets of blank paper and counting them up. Planning the design was also important so that the red lines run straight down the front legs of the table.

When covering the table lay your chosen paper out over it to the advantage of the design; move the pieces about and step back to check you will achieve a good result. I made sure that the red lines within the paper were parallel to the lines of the table and that the text was not too disturbed. I placed my paper directly across the drawer front (with its knobs removed) and then, feeling the slight ridge, cut out the drawer afterwards so as not to spoil the flow of the lettering.

COVERING THE TABLE

Paste the paper well with PVA adhesive and glue it onto the table, smoothing out all the air bubbles as you go. Place your next piece of paper to butt up to the previous one and repeat across the table. The paper will naturally curve over the table edge and slightly underneath. Tuck it smoothly under the surface and run a cutting knife around to remove excess paper; this is easier than measuring beforehand. Wrap the paper firmly around the legs, again cutting excess paper. When the table is totally covered let it dry thoroughly. If you see any missed air bubbles pin-prick them and flatten the bump. If the paper has buckled by adding water to thin the glue it will probably relax back as it dries. Apply several layers of varnish to the table, particularly the top. I varnished this table top twelve times, and gave the front and legs six coats.

DESK SET

The desk set of portfolio and pencil holder was covered in two different wrapping papers – an embossed red paper and a black marbled paper. I used the stiff cardboard from the back of an art pad, cut it slightly larger than A4 as I wished the portfolio to hold A4 paper and covered it with the red paper, turning the edges over onto the reverse side.

PORTFOLIO

Cover the inside of the portfolio with a slightly smaller contrasting paper; here the black marbled paper looks striking with the red surround. Corners often become scuffed, so adding ribbon to them not only enhances the appearance of the folder but helps make it more durable. Additional ribbon can be used to contain the papers; simply tuck the ends underneath the lining and paste them down.

PENCIL HOLDER AND PENCILS

The simple square pencil holder was made out of the off-cuts from the art pad cardboard, and covered in the same way as the portfolio. The paper scraps were then used to cover one or two pencils.

Above *Covered in plain red and black papers, the desk set tones well with the writing table on page 17.*

GLASS VASE

This glass vase is decorated with reverse découpage. I wanted it to match the writing table on page 17, so I cut out various parts of the lettering, seals and ribbon of the house deed. The red lines would define the rim of the vase. I also decided to paint the inside of the vase so that the glass would be opaque.

APPLYING THE GLUE
Brush the glue onto the face of the images and paste them inside the vase onto the glass. Add as many images as you require, then allow the glue to dry fully.

APPLYING THE PAINT
To paint the inside of a vase can be tricky, so I sponged mine by dipping a small piece of foam into red paint. With my hand inside the vase, I tapped the colour onto the inside glass with the piece of foam.

This gives a gentle application of colour and a soft effect. I sprayed at least twelve coats of varnish inside the vase as I wished to use it for flowers, and the end result looked most effective.

Reverse découpage

With this method the images are pasted behind a protective surface such as glass. If you are decorating a vase or jug you need to choose a vessel that is big enough to get your hand into. Applying varnish to the inside of a vase is also difficult, so I use a can of spray varnish.

Only red paint was used inside this reverse découpage glass vase, but interesting effects could be achieved with two tones of paint.

ℐTAMP FRAMED MIRROR

On passing a local framer's I noticed an old picture frame thrown out with the rubbish. When I asked the framer if I could take it he warned me that it was infested with woodworm. So on my walk home with the frame over my shoulder I bought a can of woodworm pesticide. At home I put the frame directly into the bath, isolating it from any wood in my flat, and proceeded to spray the pesticide into every tiny hole to recover this lovely undulating frame.

This frame was decorated with assorted stamps, but you could try using them thematically, either in related colours or pictorial subjects, such as butterflies.

SETTING TO WORK

The holes left by the woodworm had to be covered and découpage was an excellent way to do this. My small daughter needed a mirror in her room, so we raided the seconds from the stamp collection.

Usually when using anything sticky and working with a child I cover the table liberally with newspaper. However, in this case the newspaper would have stuck to the frame and all would have been confusion. So I recommend a large moist dishcloth to hand for sticky fingers and endless wiping of your kitchen or table top surface.

STICKING DOWN THE STAMPS

As the wood was in such bad condition we painted glue onto the frame to fill in a few of the woodworm holes and then a further wipe of PVA glue onto the back of the stamp as well; normally just the sticky back of unused stamps would be enough.

My daughter began on one corner and I chose the diagonal one, but I noticed that she chose all the most colourful stamps and I had to encourage her to intersperse some duller and more mundane ones in between to give a more balanced look, as the detail of Mona Lisa's smile and bright oranges demonstrates.

The frame took some hours to complete by sticking down the individual stamps one by one. However, we chatted along and Tiphaine, my daughter, looked up some of the countries in the atlas. The advantage of découpage is that you can stop at any moment and resume your work when required; it does not matter if one area dries before another. Stamps are ideal to begin with as they are easy to push

one beneath another and to smooth down, thus avoiding air bubbles. Our work finally met on one side and we interlinked our stamps, completely covering the old frame.

VARNISHING

Allow time for the PVA glue to dry thoroughly, depending on how liberally you or your helper have used the glue. Then paint the frame with PVA glue; this will seal the découpage and protect the stamps. Allow this thick layer of glue to dry thoroughly overnight. Then, using a totally clear acrylic varnish, seal the frame with two or three coats. Do not use oil-based varnish as it will yellow with age and spoil the stamps. With a mirror fitted into the frame, the final effect made a delightful addition to Tiphaine's room.

STAMP BOX

Many accessories can be decorated with used stamps and we decided to cover a small box in which to keep duplicate stamps from our collection before starting on some new découpage projects.

Finished and in place, the mirror reflects my daughter's bedroom and a photo-découpage screen that we are working on. All sorts of images can be used to decorate items large and small.

Papier mâché became popular in Europe in the nineteenth century for items such as small trinket boxes and trays, and is now enjoying a revival as a sophisticated craft medium. It is still widely used in the East for household objects. You can use a variety of ingredients for papier mâché, but the recycling of any used papers into a new creation always gives me pleasure. A versatile medium, papier mâché can be used in layers to make items such as light, translucent bowls or as pulp to build up sculptural forms and models. Much of the packaging that we throw away today is ideal for papier mâché work, as raw material or as moulds.

PAPIER MACHE

Opposite *These delightful papier mâché bowls are made from layers of tissue paper.*

STEP BY STEP
*L*AYERED PAPIER MACHE BOWLS

To create a bowl shape you need a form to follow. I find balloons practical as you can blow them up to different sizes, but you could also use a pudding bowl or a plate as a mould. I use wallpaper lining paper to make my papier mâché, but the traditional way is with newspaper. You will need three layers of lining paper or at least seven layers of newspaper since it is thinner.

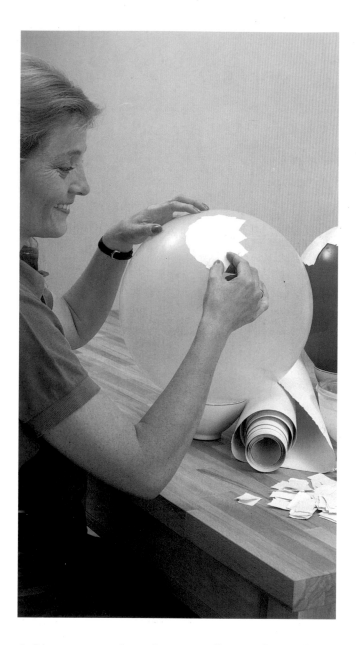

Materials

- **Wallpaper lining paper (or newspaper)**
- **Balloons of different sizes**
- **Made-up wallpaper paste**
- **Food film wrap**
- **Paperclips**
- **PVA glue**
- **Scissors**
- **Acrylic paints**
- **Acrylic varnish**

1 Rip your paper into pieces – small pieces for small bowls and larger ones for bigger bowls. Make up your wallpaper paste according to the manufacturer's instructions and place your paper pieces covered with paste directly onto the balloon mould. Begin at the top and radiate the pieces horizontally outwards, overlapping each to form a strong and uniform covering. Descend layer by layer until you have the depth of bowl you require.

When I have made up a quantity of paste I like to have several bowls on the go, so I work on three or four different sized balloons at the same time. If you need to leave your work unfinished, just cover the glued work with food film wrap to stop it drying out.

2 When adding the second layer it is important to increase the strength of the bowl by placing this layer of paper vertically over the first horizontal layer. Then cover the bowl with another layer of horizontal pieces, thus forming a woven pattern. Add further alternate layers if you are using newspaper.

3 Your work should dry overnight. When it is completely dry, ease the balloon out of the papier mâché. The interior of the bowl will still be damp, so leave it to dry naturally. For additional strength I then coat the bowl inside and out with a layer of PVA glue, which will dry to a transparent finish.

4 If the lip of your bowl has separated while drying put a little PVA glue between the paper layers and paperclip them together to dry. Decorating papier mâché bowls is great fun. I use acrylic paint because the colours are so vibrant and it is non-toxic, which is important should you want to use the bowls for food. When I have finished decorating the bowls I neaten the edges with a pair of scissors. Then, to seal my work, I apply several coats of clear, acrylic varnish.

Items made in papier mâché should be wiped clean with a light soapy rinse and dried immediately. They should never be immersed in water.

RAW-EDGED GOLD LEAF BOWLS

Gold leaf always looks sumptuous, but it is expensive and difficult to apply. However, while patchy gold leaf might look dreadful on a picture frame, it has great charm on the surface of a papier mâché bowl. The real trick is to buy the mock-metal 'gold leaf' now available in the form of a transfer on fine paper, rather like sweet wrappers. This is much easier to peel away and apply to surfaces.

Mock gold leaf is easy to apply and makes a luxurious covering for simple layered papier mâché bowls. Use them for special presents or festive occasions.

PREPARING THE BOWL

Decorate the outside of your papier mâché bowl (see page 25) with the colours you require. Then, on the inner surface to be gold leafed, paint a watered-down undercoat; some of this undercoat will show through the gold leaf. When the paint is thoroughly dry close the doors and windows to prevent draughts, turn off fan heaters and air-conditioning, and send clamouring children and cats out of the room. Anything that ruffles the air is a disaster when placing flimsy gold leaf on any item.

APPLYING GOLD LEAF

Paint a small area the same size of your gold leaf transfer with acrylic gel medium, which acts as a light type of glue or sealant. Place the gold leaf transfer over the glued area and gently remove the paper backing. If the gold leaf adheres to the paper and not to the bowl, massage the paper backing until the gold sticks to the bowl and continue to peel away the paper just as you do with children's transfers.

Leave the bowl to dry, and if you want to fill in bald areas with the tiny flakes of gold leaf left on the transfer paper you can have another go; personally I rather like the occasional broken effect. Protect your bowls with another gently applied layer of acrylic gel medium; it is lighter and finer than PVA, which might remove the gold leaf.

$\mathcal{T}$ISSUE BOWLS

The bowls shown on page 22 are made from tissue paper. They are not durable, but they are adaptable to many lighter uses for bread, biscuits and apéritif nibbles; tilting slightly on the table surface, they are invitingly tempting. Again these bowls are made over a balloon mould form, so it is a matter of choosing the right size of balloon for your required bowl. All these bowls can be made in a few hours.

Blow up balloons of varying sizes and spray them with water so that the tissue paper does not temporarily slither about. Cover the balloon with a whole sheet of tissue paper and then decorate. This decoration will show on the inside of your bowl and there are many variations.

MAKING THE BLUE BOWL

1 The blue bowl has strips of blue tissue over the first layer of white tissue and as the tissue is moist it bleeds blue dye into the glue for an interesting veined effect.

2 Add another layer of tissue paper and brush with glue. Repeat the process until you have four to six layers. Leave to dry. Remove the balloon and paint the inside of the bowl with PVA glue. Finally varnish.

Design ideas

You can use small pieces of tin foil or sweet wrappers or perhaps even a torn-up letter as decoration. Threads of wire, cotton, wool or string can be used to create any number of patterns. If you want your design on the outside of the bowl, simply add the decoration to the last layer of the bowl.

I have used pink threads twirled into a spiral. Just cover the tissue lightly with glue and bend your cotton into it forming a pattern.

The yellow and white bowl on page 22 is made in the same way as the blue one. The small orange bowl is made from orange tissue paper with cubes of blue used as decoration just around the rim. The larger yellow bowl has yellow tissue covered with contrasting blue and red threads running over the bowl as a mock check. The largest bowl has tissue biscuit wrappers sealed within and an etched butterfly hovering inside it.

RED AND WHITE BOWLS WITH RIMS

Many years ago I was given a hand-embroidered table cloth, and bought some red cups to match. Making toning papier mâché bowls that picked out some of the design elements of the cloth gave me a welcoming and dressed table. Friends with young children often pop by for tea, and if little people tumble about with a papier mâché bowl of goodies, no harm can be done to them or the bowls.

ADDING A RIM

Follow steps 1 to 3 on pages 24–25 for making your bowl, then snip neatly around the bowl's edge to remove stray papers. To make the rims for the bowls you will need to cut out a cardboard template. Place the bowl upside down onto a piece of cardboard and draw around it. Snip out the circle from the cardboard and decide the rim shape you want. I like to vary my rim choices, so I have made a wide additional circle, a scallop edge and a wave rim. Squares, triangles and star shapes would also work well.

Attach the rim to the bowl with additional layers of papier mâché both on top and beneath the rim for strength, and just covering the raw edge of the cardboard rim, to complete the texture of the bowl. When thoroughly dry cover the rim liberally with PVA glue for additional durability and, when dry, paint your decoration on.

DECORATING THE RIMS

I find when designing that I sometimes get stuck on the decoration because my ideas are too complicated. It is best to use simple patterns. I have based these designs on cross-stitch embroidery and painted crosses around the rim of the bowl. On the next bowl I formed the crosses into circles. The fan leaf stitch on the tablecloth was simple to copy in paint around the rim of the bowl.

NAPKIN RINGS

Matching napkin rings were made by putting papier mâché over a cardboard tube, scalloping and waving the edges. I then painted the rings in contrasting red, picking out design details in white to complete the table setting.

Each of these bowls has a different shaped rim with different decoration, but painted in red they coordinate well as a set.

I decided to cover my ark to tone in with the animals, using bright and vibrant colours from my imagination.

NOAH'S ARK AND ANIMALS

One of the joys of papier mâché is covering something as simple as a piece of cardboard and transforming it into a quite different item. This Noah's Ark was made from a shoe box that I cut up. The sides made a good cabin, particularly when windows were cut through, and the top and bottom of the box were stuck together and painted to form the roof, topped by a cardboard chimney. The ark was taped into a cardboard hull.

USING REFERENCE

All the tape, glue and any over-lapping pieces of cardboard are covered with layers of coloured tissue paper. The animals are made from twisted wire. I find that even for the most simple slithering snake, it is essential to have a good illustration available. As for the elephant you just get a little more movement for the animal's natural characteristics if you follow some reference. As you see, my baby elephant is not a work of art but, thanks to studying a picture, he *is* an elephant.

MAKING THE ANIMALS

Fold a piece of thin wire around onto itself, using pliers for the more intricate angles. The structure does not have to be very strong; it is really just an armature to rest the tissue paper strips on. Apply the tissue strips over the wire frame and gradually build up the shape of the animal. Add pieces to describe the character of the animal – a twist of tissue is ideal for the elephant's tail, ruffled tissue perfect for the lion's mane.

Glue all the tissue paper firmly with PVA glue, and add an additional coat when the animal is finished. When thoroughly dry, coat with a layer of varnish. Six-year-olds and older children would enjoy helping to make animals of their own.

Above *The animals are easy to make from wire, but should not be given to a very young child for safety reasons.*

Below *The finished elephant, painted and varnished, with a dot for an eye.*

Other toys and models

Layered papier mâché and cardboard can be used to create many other items, such as a Christmas crib with stable and animals, a doll's house, a station, a castle; there are endless possibilities.

𝒫ULP PAPIER MACHE

Papier mâché using pulp is more messy and takes longer than the layered method, but it is an ideal modelling material for more sculptured items. It can be used to shape a variety of items from mirror frames to models such as the sculptured pig, which is described step by step on pages 34–35.

By varying the ingredients of papier mâché pulp you can make a material that is very strong, and providing there is a supporting armature you can even make simple and inexpensive furniture by recycling paper. Here is a basic recipe for making pulp.

The shape of the pig's tail is easy to form by bending chicken wire and then covering it with pulp papier mâché. It is added on separately to the body of the animal when the main structure has been covered with papier mâché.

To make 1 litre (2 pints) of pulp

Four double-page sheets of broadsheet newspaper

30 ml (2 tablespoons) of whiting or plaster of Paris

30 ml (2 tablespoons) of PVA glue

15 ml (1 tablespoon) of linseed oil (optional, but makes pulp easier to work)

Two drops of oil of wintergreen or oil of cloves (optional, but prevents papier mâché rotting)

30 ml (2 tablespoons) of dry wallpaper paste

MAKING PULP PAPIER MACHE
Tear the paper in the direction of the grain into 2.5 cm (1 in) squares and soak in a bucket of water overnight. Then boil the paper for twenty minutes in 2 litres (3 ½ pints) of water. When cool transform the paper into pulp in a food processor. Strain the pulp into a sieve, shaking out the surplus water.

Put the pulp into a large airtight container and add the whiting or plaster of Paris, the PVA glue, linseed oil and oil of wintergreen or oil of cloves. Mix thoroughly. If you want a stronger solution add wallpaper paste. If you are working with children check that the wallpaper paste does not contain a pesticide; many do. The pulp will store well in an airtight container for up to a month in a cool place. After that it begins to get a little too smelly to want to use.

Opposite *Pulp papier mâché is ideal for modelled items. Instructions for making the pig are overleaf, and details of how to make the shaped mirrors are on pages 36–37.*

STEP BY STEP
*P*ULP PAPIER MACHE PIG

This pig is made by using papier mâché pulp over a chicken-wire structure. The job of applying the pulp to the frame is a messy one, so I work outside on the terrace. If you are working indoors you need to protect your work surface not only from bits of wet pulp but also from sharp pieces of wire, such as the pig's trotters, which might scratch.

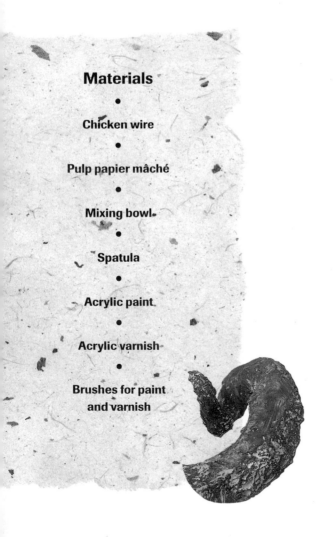

Materials

•

Chicken wire

•

Pulp papier mâché

•

Mixing bowl

•

Spatula

•

Acrylic paint

•

Acrylic varnish

•

Brushes for paint and varnish

1 Make up your frame using chicken wire, making sure that your structure is very firm. Interlink as many of the raw chicken-wire edges as possible, both to strengthen the frame and to protect your hands; a raw wire can cut you badly. Leave the tail area open and also the snout. The pulp is best pressed from both sides; I put one of my hands inside the pig so that all the pulp being applied does not fall right through.

2 Wait until the top of the pig has totally dried, then you can turn him onto his back and complete his legs and tummy, otherwise all the pulp will fall off. Gravity will help the pulp stay in place until dry. I returned to the pig throughout a week filling in little areas.

3 I found two large bulbous beads and sunk them into the pulp as eyes, building up the pulp as natural sockets. On finishing the main body of the pig the tail can now be attached by wiring it on firmly. Also bend the chicken wire in firmly to make the shape of the snout with an upturned snuffling nose. Apply the pulp to the tail and snout, building in expression. The advantage of pulp is that you can always add a little more to get the shape right. Pulp does tend to sink as it dries so you can be generous in your application.

4 The final step is to paint the pig. I chose a brownish pink colour and varied the tones over the pig's body, giving him dirty trotters and a lighter back where pigs scratch themselves. Use acrylic paints for a durable, colour-fast finish with numerous layers of varnish as protection so that you can leave the pig outside for the summer.

MIRRORS

Small pieces of broken mirror are embedded in this heart-shaped frame made from pulp papier mâché. The full frame is pictured on page 33.

These small mirrors are an easy pulp papier mâché project to tackle. On finding a broken mirror I decided to break it up into smaller pieces and these determined the shapes of my frames.

If you require special shapes for your mirrors it is advisable to use glass cutters, which are readily available. Even so, while it is easy to cut a straight line, you may find cutting curves laborious. I recommend that you wear protective gloves when breaking glass and make sure that you do not leave splinters.

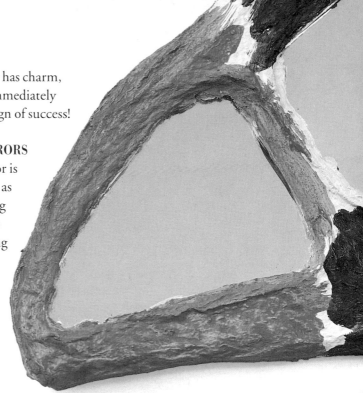

HEART MIRROR

The heart was an obvious shape to make. I firmly glued the mirror to a square of strong cardboard and built up the pulp around it. The pulp stuck well to the mirror, thus enclosing and hiding the raw edge of the mirror. Papier mâché pulp sinks as it dries, so my first application looked rather mean.

I found the little fragments of mirror at the bottom of my box so it was happy chance that with my second application of pulp I could sink them into the pulp enclosing the raw edges. When the heart pulp frame was thoroughly dry I cut the shape out of the cardboard base with a strong-bladed craft knife, and then decorated the pulp with red acrylic paint. The heart form is very rough and ready but to me it has charm, and my children all immediately wanted one – a sure sign of success!

FISH AND STAR MIRRORS

The leaping fish mirror is made in the same way as the heart, firmly gluing the mirror pieces onto cardboard and building the pulp around, enclosing all raw mirror edges.

The variations on these shaped mirrors are endless. My daughter Abigail began the star frame and built up the pulp into peaks, which gave a different dimension to the piece.

Above *Detail of the fish frame on page 33. The sharp edges of the mirror are hidden under the papier mâché.*

Left *This star mirror shows how easy it is to model papier mâché into shapes.*

Decorative printing can be applied to a large range of materials and there are many different techniques you can use. Here I shall show you how to make and use simple stencils, stamps and linocuts. The projects include lampshades, boxes, stationery and wrapping paper, and the effects can be so pleasing that once you have begun you will not want to stop. I find the temptation to continue printing everything in sight, including curtains, cushions and walls, can be too much to contain and it is easy to get carried away. Keep the patterns simple and use few colours to start with to achieve maximum impact.

PRINTING

Opposite *Stencils with a simple motif are a stylish way of personalizing home accessories.*

STEP BY STEP
$\mathcal{S}$TENCILLED FLOWER

Flowers are a universal theme and the simple design of this chinoiserie stencil can be used for decoration throughout your home. Using your stencil can sometimes be rather daunting at first, whether you are printing a postcard, stationery or full-scale home accessories such as a lamp or curtains. Try your stencil technique out on spare paper and if you do not like the effect you can always have another go.

1 Trace off the flower and bud stencil pattern at the back of the book. Then transfer the stencil design onto oiled manila paper, readily available from art shops. If your traced outline is faint on the oiled manila go over it again with a soft pencil.

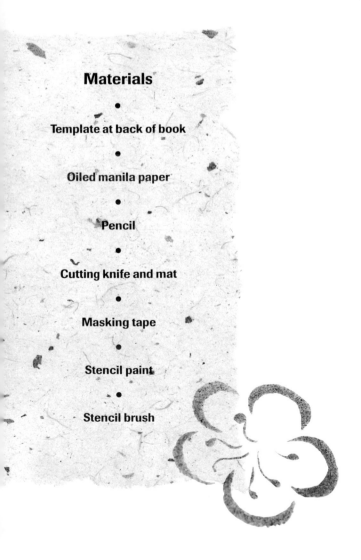

Materials

•

Template at back of book

•

Oiled manila paper

•

Pencil

•

Cutting knife and mat

•

Masking tape

•

Stencil paint

•

Stencil brush

2 Then, using a cutting knife and mat, cut out the flowers, buds and stem motifs by pulling the knife firmly along the traced outline. When cutting hold the manila paper with one hand to keep the paper still and cut away from this hand in case the knife slips.

3 Attach the cut stencil to your chosen paper with masking tape to avoid any movement while you work. Load your stencil brush with a small amount of paint. Dab the brush on a spare piece of paper to check that it is not overloaded. Gently apply the paint to the stencil using a quick dabbing motion, holding the brush upright. The tip of a stencil brush is cut blunt to avoid accidentally painting under the edges of the stencil.

4 If you want to apply more than one colour use a different brush for each as washing your brush will add water, causing the paint to seep beneath the stencil. When you have finished peel back the stencil to reveal the stencilled image. If you require a stronger image apply more paint, replacing the stencil in the same position for a crisply defined edge.

STENCILLED ACCESSORIES

Stencilling is a most efficient way of printing on many different surfaces and enables you to coordinate decoration on furnishings using the same technique. The items on page 38 show just effective a simple theme can look. Here you can use an old lampshade as a pattern for a new paper stencilled one and transform a shoe box into an attractive stationery box to contain matching paper and envelopes with a single motif.

LAMPSHADE

Spread out your old shade over your chosen new paper and trace around it; you might have to weight it down as it will tend to curl after years as a shade. Place the stencil onto the new lampshade piece, taping it down, and apply the stencil paint. If there are any parts of the stencil design that you do not wish to use mask them off with tape. I usually lift up the stencil carefully to have a peek at what will be stencilled.

On the lampshade on page 38 I have stencilled the bottom rim of the shade and cut around the flowers to enhance the stencil print.

STATIONERY BOX

A shoe box takes on a new lease of life with thick paper covering it. I used watercolour paper to cover the box as I like its texture.

To measure the paper, just mark around the bottom and four sides of the box onto your chosen paper – the pattern will be like a splayed-out cross. Then do the same for the lid, adding 2.5 cm (1 in) or so all round. For the lid, I stencilled the edge with flowers and cut around the

individual forms to enhance them and match the lampshade. While gluing down the paper lid pattern I left the side panels free, giving a skirt appearance to the box and further softening its familiar lines.

Some stencilled notepaper and envelopes completed the stationery box.

Making lampshades

Lampshades are very easy to make and there is a wide range of thicker cards and decorative papers from which to choose. For a large shade the weight of the paper should be 250 gsm (140 lb); for a smaller shade, such as the blue one shown here 140 gsm (65 lb); for very small ones, or if you do not require the shade to be long lasting, 90 gsm (40 lb) or even 60 gsm (30 lb) will do. Be aware of the proximity of the bulb to the paper; leave at least 7 cm (3 in) between the two — the higher the wattage, the greater the distance.

Stencilled stationery adds a personal touch to letters and notes, and makes an unusual small gift.

A single stencil can be used for a variety of effects and interpreted to your own requirements. This lampshade tones with a reverse découpage glass base.

LAMP AND TONING BASE

The blue lampshade is stencilled with the full stencil of flowers in white. The lamp base is a converted glass vase into which I could just squeeze my hand. I printed stencils on paper, cut out the motifs and glued them with PVA adhesive face down to the interior of the glass vase as described for reverse découpage on page 19.

When the flowers are dry, sponge a little white paint over the

back of the design, giving a cloudy effect and making the glass opaque. Special light fittings are available from lamp suppliers to convert vases into lamps.

PRINTING ONTO FABRIC

Light filters through the curtain on page 38, which I decorated using the full stencil, repeating it back and forth to make a deep border. I used fabric paint so that the curtain is fully washable and practical.

43

MAKING PRINTING STAMPS

Many ready-made printing stamps can be bought, but it is easy to make your own. Over the next four pages I show you how to make two basic types of stamps that can be used to add interesting and individual decoration to items such as files, folders, wrapping paper and greetings cards.

STAMPS AND LINOCUTS

One of the simplest methods is to stick shapes and textures onto a stiff cardboard backing. Ordinary packaging materials are fine for this. Wrapping string over a cardboard shape or gluing string onto cardboard creates an effective design ready for use in no time at all. Linocuts are also quick and easy to do and again the simplest design can look quite stunning.

PRINTING

I apply the paint to the stamp with a roller as this gives a more even covering and I use water-based block printing colours as the paint dries quickly. However, the traditional method is to use oil-based inks and you may prefer the slightly richer effect that they give. The textures of all printing blocks and linocuts vary as you print each image by hand, which gives a diverse and sometimes unpredictable overall design.

I tend to use printing stamps in a haphazard 'scatter' pattern, but if you want a repeating design be sure to measure out carefully on the item you are printing. In either case it is worth checking the effect of your stamp on a spare piece of paper before you set to in earnest.

Storing linocuts

If you wash your linocuts well you can store them flat under pressure to avoid curling and reuse them indefinitely.

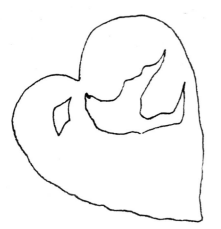
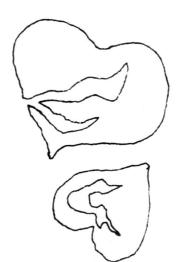

Above *These 'heart' stencils can be traced or photocopied and used to make linocuts (see pages 48–49).*

Opposite *Simple stamps and linocuts have been used here to print decoration on brown paper to cover files, folders and other basic stationery.*

STEP BY STEP
*S*TRING STAMP PRINTING

*These string stamps are inexpensive to make,
with their basic components of string and
cardboard. Cereal boxes or the back of a
notepaper pad that you would normally
throw away can be recycled to produce unusual
decorative details. Vary the shapes – rectangles,
squares, circles and triangles – and cut out
holes in the middle of some of them.
The string can also be used to make
interesting outline patterns.*

Materials

- Packaging cardboard
- String
- PVA glue
- Pins
- Block printing colours
- Tile or flat non-absorbent surface to roll out the paint on
- Lino roller to suit the size of your design

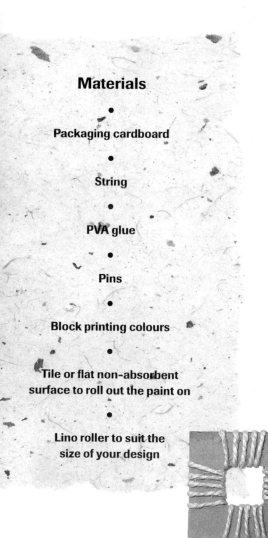

1 Cut up some packaging cardboard to use as the base for the stamps. If you are cutting shapes with holes in the centre just wrap the string around the forms and glue it in place. With the shapes without holes you can create a variety of outline patterns. Cover the card with a thick layer of PVA glue, then form your string into a design in it. My string was a little springy, so I tacked the design down temporarily with pins until the glue dried.

2 Roll out the paint on the tile or flat non-absorbent surface, thoroughly covering the roller. Then roll the paint onto the raised string that will form the design. Initially you will need to apply several layers of paint as the string is porous and will absorb a quantity of paint.

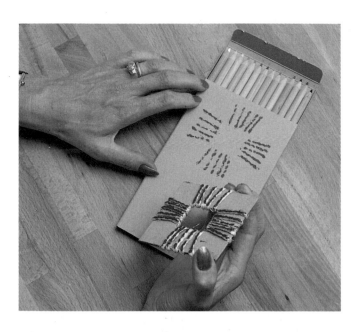

3 Print out the string template by holding the stamp firmly at the sides and pressing down. With the forms that have a hole in the middle and string wound all the way around, you could use the reverse side for a contrasting colour without having to make a new stamp.

4 The string stamps printed in bright primary colours look especially effective when used to decorate ordinary brown paper items, giving inexpensive carriers and folders individual style. Some ideas for string outline patterns might be spirals, swirls, stars, hearts, crosses or fishes.

STEP BY STEP
*L*INOCUT PRINTING

The linocut has been used by many artists to create images and illustrations. Lino has an even surface and is easily worked. You can produce your own miniature work of art to print decoration on paper goods such as notelets, greetings cards, wrapping paper and gift tags. Here I have chosen to make a simple heart-shaped stamp. All the materials are readily available at art suppliers.

1 Draw the image you want directly onto the lino, or transfer a tracing. If you are designing a letter remember to draw it in mirror image. If your mark is faint go over it in felt-tip pen. Then, with the lino cutter, gouge out the section of the design that you do not want to print – the remaining lino will give the printed design when paint is applied to it. Be careful that you do not nick your fingers with the cutter.

Materials

- **Piece of lino**

- **Block printing colours (I have used Cadmium Red for the heart)**

- **Lino roller to suit the size of your design**

- **Lino cutter, often supplied with varying shapes of cutting blades**

- **Tile or flat non-absorbent surface to roll out the paint on**

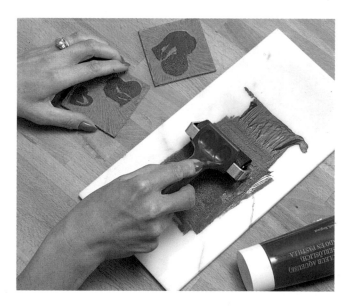

2 Squeeze out the block printing paint onto the tile or flat non-absorbent surface and roll the roller back and forth in long movements so that the roller is totally covered. Transfer the paint to the lino in firm rolling motions. Roll back and forth to apply the paint thickly for a dense print, or only once for a lighter image.

3 Reverse the lino over the paper and place firmly into position. Holding the lino firmly with one hand to avoid movement, press down and smooth the side of your hand over the back of the lino, applying pressure. You can also use the back of a wooden spoon to apply pressure; it depends on how large the linocut is and how many lino prints you want to make.

4 Separate out your work to dry. Since I have a small work area I overlap the cards while the paint is still tacky. To dry large sheets of paper I use a freestanding clothes drier or towel rail and on sunny days I have pegged them up on a washing line – the paper looks wonderful drying in the breeze. These hearts make charming tags with a toning thread attached and look distinctive when cut out for someone special.

PRINTED PAPER

Printed decoration can transform even the dullest item, as the wrapping paper, box files and envelopes on page 45 show. Do not discard paper that could be given an extended lease of life – for instance, creased brown paper can be recycled and gives exciting results when printed with bright colours. If you are making your own carriers or boxes from the templates on pages 68 and 69 it is best to print the paper first and then make up the items.

Here is a variety of presents, cards and hand-painted and printed wrapping papers. You can design the paper to fit the occasion, whether birthday, anniversary or Christmas.

PLACING THE STAMPS

One box file on page 45 is printed in blue with a round string stamp. To print over the corner of a book or file like this place the stamp firmly on one side and apply pressure for it to print; then, without moving the stamp, balance it over onto the next side and press firmly to print over the corner and complete the pattern of the stamp. The small file is printed with the same motif, as is the pencil box, where only half the stamp has been applied.

The other box file is printed on the spine only with the heart linocut on pages 48-49. Notice how each motif has printed slightly differently, producing an interesting uneven texture on the paper. Hearts are always a popular design and ideal to print across the flap of an envelope hiding romantic secrets within, perhaps for a special Valentine message.

CARDS AND TISSUE PAPER

I made a slightly larger linocut for the fishes used on the greetings cards. I sketched the fish onto the lino in pencil first, then firmed up the design in felt-tip pen. Before removing any lino it is sometimes useful to shade the area that you are cutting away so that you can envisage the final effect. I gouged away the sea area with a curved lino cutter and also the fishes' eyes and backbones. The design was printed onto A5 size paper folded in half to make personalized greetings cards.

After printing the cards I decided to print some matching tissue paper in which to wrap a gift. On a thin material such as this the paint can give an almost embossed effect. It is usually enough to apply pressure to the linocut just with your thumb to achieve the effect.

VEGETABLE PRINTS

Vegetable prints are probably the easiest of all to make, yet can give some surprisingly sophisticated results. Simply cut a potato in half and draw your chosen image onto the flat surface in felt-tip pen. Cut away the remainder of the flesh of the potato and you have an effective printing stamp. The yellow suns on the red paper present on page 50 were produced in this way.

Experiment with your vegetables – onions produce an interesting textured finish and carrots are ideal for intricate designs.

Trace or photocopy the fish motif to make your own linocut to use for printing greetings cards as shown on pages 48–49. Experiment with different colours, perhaps mixing them on the tile as you roll to create a gradated effect.

Light filtering through paper gives a delightful effect, one that the Japanese in particular have perfected with artistic understatement. It is surprising how easy it is to make attractive patterns simply with tiny cuts. As sunlight or artificial light pushes it way through these spaces it casts interesting shadows and the tiniest pinpricks create changes of texture over a sheet of paper in a way that is reminiscent of traditional tinwork. Assorted cuts, slits and holes can be used to decorate diverse paper items, from lampshades to window blinds, from wrapping paper to silhouettes. There are some unusual candle shades here for you to create, but do make sure you never leave lighted candles unattended.

CUTTING AND PIERCING

Opposite *The old-fashioned art of silhouettes makes a charming family display.*

STEP BY STEP
SILHOUETTES

Here is an easy way to make silhouettes by simply drawing the outline of your subject and filling it in with black ink. You can then decide to cut it out in the traditional way or to draw in a decorative background as in the framed pictures on page 52, thus removing the possibility of making any mistakes when cutting out. Try full-length poses as well as portrait heads of family and friends.

1 I have used family photographs as my source material. I rummaged through a large box full of discarded photographs looking for those taken in profile. There were not many as people are usually snapped face on, but from those I found I selected the ones that would make the most interesting for silhouettes. Simply trace over the top of your photograph, picking out any details such as a ribbon in the hair, a curl, or whiskers on the cat.

Materials

•
Profile photographs or pictures cut from a magazine
•
Tracing paper
•
Pencil
•
Mounting board or thick smooth paper
•
Fine black felt-tip pen
•
Thick black felt-tip pen

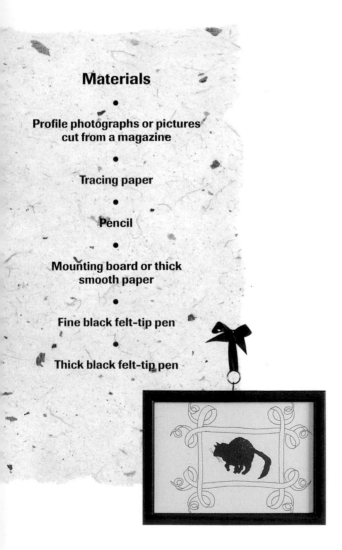

2 Trace out the image onto mounting board or good, thick, smooth paper. It will be a mirror image of the photograph, but if you want the profile to face the same way just trace your tracing and transfer that to your chosen surface.

3 Remove the tracing and go over the traced pencil line on the mounting board with a fine black felt-tip pen. Try to keep your hand steady, or you might draw an additional bump in the nose of your subject as I did when drawing my son!

Framing the silhouettes

Classic small black frames are available from most large department stores. To add a little variety and some decorative style I removed the metal fixtures from behind the frames and made them into a feature. I placed them on top of the frames and made a tiny hole to screw each one into. Black ribbons completed the hangings and when the pictures were tacked and grouped together they made a rather elegant setting above a small table offset by silverware.

4 Then, using a thicker black felt-tip pen, fill in the image with precise markings back and forth to cover the outlined space. To complete the silhouette trace out the ribbon or panel images at the back of the book and trace them onto the silhouette paper, making sure that the silhouette is in the centre. Then outline the traced ribbon or panel with a thin black felt-tip pen. Use a soft eraser to remove any pencil lines from around the silhouette or background image.

Alternatively, cut out a rectangle around your chosen border from the back of the book. Then cut out around the outline of the silhouette and paste it down in the centre of the border ready for framing.

$\mathscr{P}$IERCED AND SLIT CANDLE SHADES

Candle shades give a soft light and create an intimate atmosphere, but lighted candles can be dangerous and they should not be left unattended. I recently presented some candle shades I had made to an American friend who politely used them that evening: the air conditioning caused havoc. So please be careful and test your interior beforehand. Always use straight-sided candles in the shades and the correct brass adapter, and keep them away from draughts.

PIERCED CANDLE SHADE

One of the quickest forms of decoration to apply to a lampshade is to make a series of pierced lines using the sewing machine.
Use the template pattern on page 58. Cut your lampshade from the paper of your choice; for such a small shade a paper weight of 60 gsm (30 lb) or 90 gsm (40 lb) is adequate.

Then, remove the thread from your machine and, using an old blunt needle, follow the line of the shade. Next, position the sewing-machine foot against the pierced line and progress up the shade. You can vary the length of stitch used; I lengthened mine to the maximum and then reduced it slightly for a variety of effects. You could also try using totally different stitch patterns if your machine has them, adding a new dimension to your decorative piercing.

SLIT WINDOW CANDLE SHADE

The middle candle shade is decorated with small windows opening out in the form of triangles, squares and rectangles; these smart and contemporary-looking shades are quick to cut using a cutting knife and mat. The template on page 58 has some triangles for you to follow.

Mark out the shape on the reverse. Then cut the shapes, remembering not to cut one side, which is all too easy to do by accident – to remind myself I do not draw the last side in. Having cut the forms, gently push them through onto the right side of the lamp. When the candle is lit the light will flow through the tiny windows and cast flickering shadows.

SCALLOPED CANDLE SHADE

The small scalloped candle shade is a favourite of mine; its simple style nestles happily into any interior, be it contemporary or classical. Both the jaunty small scallops at the top and the larger ones at the base of the shade are accentuated by the use of piercing. Make these holes with a hat pin or large needle and follow the scalloped form around to give greater definition to the shape.

Opposite *Any number of delicate patterns can be traced and pierced into candle shades. Cut pictorial designs also look attractive when illuminated by the soft glow of a lit candle.*

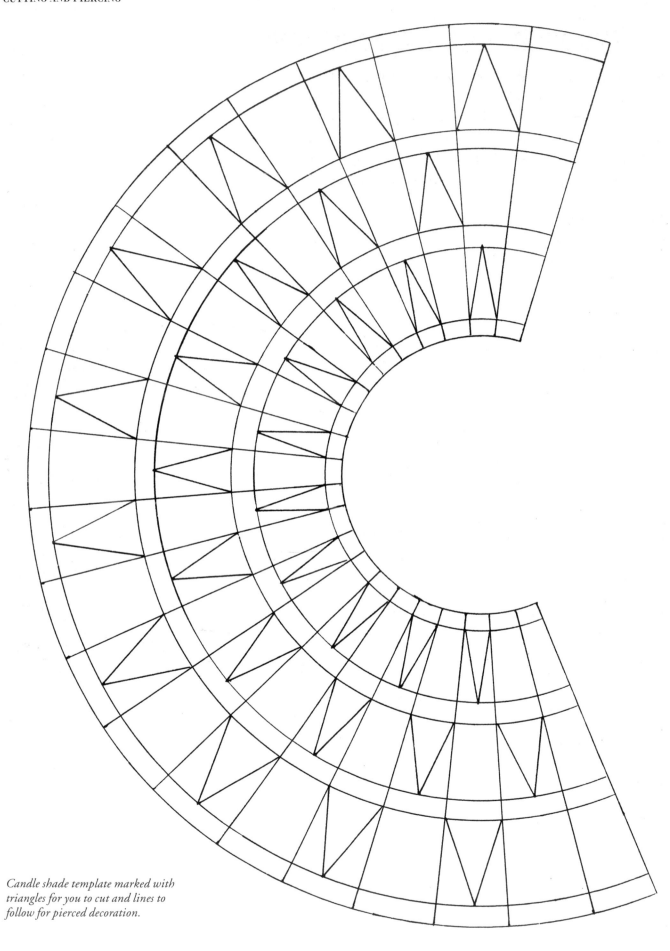

Candle shade template marked with triangles for you to cut and lines to follow for pierced decoration.

𝒮TAMP ADVENT CALENDAR CANDLE SHADES

So often it is a simple idea that makes a successful and timeless decoration. Little lamps like these were a part of my childhood. I had completely forgotten about them, but while making a very neat and clean windowed shade, something made me put a stamp behind an opening and hold it up to the light. Treasures like these shades are not to everyone's taste, but they are especially popular with children.

WINDOW ON THE PAST

I raided my daughters' stamp collection, and again discovered time looking over my shoulder at my childhood and theirs as I turned over the stamps in my hands. Some I remembered, other required prompting. Exquisitely designed stamps are produced each year all over the world and are a reminder of how quickly time flies.

MAKING THE SHADE

Place the selected stamps around the shade; put the larger ones at the base and the smaller ones at the top to balance the proportions. Just mark around the stamp in pencil on the reverse of the shade and cut slightly within this mark, remembering to cut only the top and bottom edges. Then cut firmly down the middles of the rectangles for the shutters.

Paste gently around the white perforated edge of each stamp with PVA glue, and place it carefully behind its allotted window space. I leave some windows open, and others closed. However, I have noticed at the end of a dinner party that all the windows have been opened; so there is a little of the child in even the sternest adult.

A novel way to use Christmas stamps decoratively. The candle lights up the pictures when the shutters to the tiny windows are opened.

$\mathscr{P}$IERCED BLIND

One of my roller blinds looked a little tired, so I decided to replace it by making one out of pierced paper. Initially I had a problem in finding large rolls of paper that were wide enough; wallpaper is too narrow for most windows. However, I tracked down a specialist paper shop where I found wide rolls of 150 gsm (70 lb) that were exceptionally inexpensive and in every conceivable colour; so it is worth looking around if at first you cannot find what you need.

MAKING THE BLIND

The only other problem I found in making this blind is that it is so simple that it became rather boring to complete, but the results are worth it. All you need is the longest ruler you can find or two smaller ones taped together, a small metal eyelet punch available from most hardware shops, a hammer and a DIY roller blind kit.

First measure the width and depth of your window to check that your paper is the right size. Place the punch where you want a hole and tap the punch on the end with a hammer to make the hole. In order to obtain long straight and measured lines I laid the ruler across the paper, which was cascading over both sides of my table, punching holes as my pattern required. You might find it easier, especially if you are planning a complicated design, to measure out your pattern, marking in pencil where you want the holes to be before you actually start punching. The roller blind kit is easy to assemble following the manufacturer's instructions.

Ideas to try…

Although I am pleased with my blind I now feel that I could have been more adventurous with my pattern. Rather than punching a geometric design, perhaps initials would have been more intimate; a large cockerel chasing a hen would have been amusing; or as this is the bathroom, outlines of the back scrubber, a large bar of soap or perhaps the outline of a person emerging from the bath. I impatiently await the blind becoming worn, as I shall have fun replacing it with a new and unusual design.

This paper roller blind is made from a basic DIY kit and decorated with punched holes in whatever design you choose.

$\mathcal{G}$IFT WRAPS

There are so many ways to make plain paper look interesting and add extra style to a special gift. Here I have contrasted black and white papers to give a dramatic and sophisticated effect to presents. The stitched papers can also be used for covering books and smaller pieces can be made into matching gift tags with a variety of different coloured threads.

STITCHED PAPER

'Test your stitch before you work', I can recall my mother telling me. Often I am working on just a small repair and do not have any spare fabric available. So I test my stitch on paper, and of course the effect is so engaging that I continue, making pierced stitched papers for wrapping paper or for covering small notebooks. You can vary the stitch decoration, and try stitched writing for the titles of notebooks for recipes, gardening or baby memories. Personalize wrappings and tags with initials or small messages. I usually enjoy myself experimenting with stitching so much that often the small repair that I was going to mend is put back into the sewing basket for another time.

PUNCHED PAPER

Hole punches are easy to use for quick results. Fold your paper and punch along the creased line, and then again along the fold; then flatten that fold and make another.

You can decorate the paper by threading colourful ribbon, cottons, string or twigs through the holes. I used white paper and threaded black ribbon through; by not pulling the ribbon tightly you can achieve a padded three-dimensional effect.

CLIPPED CONCERTINA PAPER

The larger present is doubly wrapped, first in white paper, then in black. The black paper is folded back and forth in a concertina and both sides of the folds are clipped with a pair of scissors, removing little triangles of paper. When the paper is opened the triangles form a diamond shape. I remember doing these paper cuts at nursery school, and my children came home with the same 'gift', so have the children join in.

You can create many assorted items by folding and weaving paper.
The book contains some simple photograph frames, a small lampshade and
four small boxes that I hope you will enjoy folding and making up to keep
or give as gifts. As a small child I remember weaving baskets, and found the
process of cutting strips of paper and weaving them very soothing.
It is fun to design containers for your own requirements in your favourite
colours. Here I show you how to make a woven filing tray, tall basket and
woven wastepaper basket to go with a child's cardboard desk and chair,
to complete a study desk for a small person.

WEAVING AND FOLDING

Opposite *Woven or folded paper can be used to make*
quite sturdy items that children will love.

STEP BY STEP
*W*OVEN WASTEPAPER BASKET

Contrasting primary colours are a joy to work and you can produce vibrant and diverse boxes and bins of all shapes and sizes just by weaving strips of paper. I made this basket for a child's desk set, but it would be equally suitable for an adult and would add a bit of colour to anyone's office or study. The design possibilities and uses for woven baskets are endless.

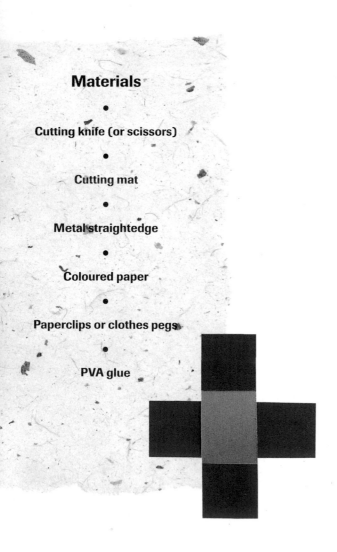

Materials

- **Cutting knife (or scissors)**
- **Cutting mat**
- **Metal straightedge**
- **Coloured paper**
- **Paperclips or clothes pegs**
- **PVA glue**

1 Cut full-length strips of varying colours of paper in the width you require. The length should be enough for the base and the two sides. For small boxes 150 gsm (70 lb) paper would be an adequate weight. For larger baskets or those destined for more robust purpose use 300 gsm (140 lb) paper. Weave the base of the waste-paper basket by laying the paper strips flat and placing contrasting strips at right angles across, weaving them in and out, and up and down, to form a woven mesh.

2 Fold the paper strands back over the base of the basket, retaining a straight basket base edge. These folded-back uprights will then make the walls of the basket and determine its height. As you will see, I have used a contrasting red for the walls of the basket to demonstrate more clearly what to do, but combine your colours as you wish.

3 To weave the basket walls attach one end of a red paper to the upright green or blue strands using a paper-clip or clothes peg. The basket is a rather floppy structure at this stage, but do not be deterred; it will soon grow. Weave the red paper in and out of the blue and green upright supports and when you have completed the woven level attach both ends of the red strip together with staples, glue or tape, trimming away excess red paper. Build up the basket sides, weaving in and out, to the height you require.

4 Finish off the top of the woven basket by folding back the upright paper strands – in this case the green and blue ones. There are several ways of finishing off the basket. Either glue the ends down or staple them back on themselves or, as shown here, bend them into and beneath the lower basket weave. Weave the interior paper strands into the lower basket weave as well and the basket is finished.

CUSTOM-MADE BASKETS

Vary your baskets with thin and thicker strips of paper and build your designs to suit specific purposes. Weaving paper is a versatile and relaxing craft, and so easy and safe to do that even small children can participate. As you become more adept you can plan quite complicated designs with different colourways, making a number of matching items.

TALL YELLOW BASKET
The yellow basket on page 62 is made with narrow strips that are 1 cm (½ in) wide. The base is seven strips wide square and is made of three yellow, one blue and three yellow, by three yellow, one blue, one yellow, one blue and finally one yellow. The basket is eleven yellow strips high, giving a tall thin basket for rulers and long scissors.

FILE TRAY
The file tray on page 62 is made of wider strips of varying widths and a mixture of colours – red, blue, yellow and green. Often the basket sizes are determined by paper length. If a large basket is required you may need to join heavy gauge 300 gsm (140 lb) paper together, using double stapling for strength.

VARIATIONS
Weaving with other paper materials is also interesting. Select colourful cardboard boxes when you go shopping; banana boxes in particular are often thick, reasonably clean and have delightful bright designs. Use a heavy tool-cutting knife and long metal straightedge to cut them into strips and weave them into very strong picnic boxes, wastepaper bins, laundry baskets or toy boxes.

For table decorations weave light papers together and include

strings, metal or fibres for added textural effects. Small baskets are ideal for crisps and biscuits at children's parties, and special containers woven in white and gold with luxury papers to hold nibbles will add an individual touch at weddings. Easter baskets containing small chocolate eggs are waiting to be found – the list of ideas for woven baskets is endless.

A close-up of the woven baskets shows how stunning the final effect can look when the positions of the coloured strips are carefully planned.

GIFT BOXES

The small boxes at the back of the book have been designed for you to cut out and fold. You could use them to contain a small gift for a friend or keep them yourself – they are ideal for trinkets or sweets. Each box is made up in a similar way, giving a firm base that will not open when goodies are placed inside.

ROSEBUDS AND RIBBONS

Cut out the template page at the back of the book, then cut out the boxes using a cutting knife and mat or embroidery scissors. Fold each box along the natural fold lines to make a cube-shaped box. Then press the folds into the base flaps so that each box will have a neat base. To make the boxes up, first attach the side flaps to the inside with a little glue. Leave to dry; you can secure the boxes with paper clips while the glue dries. When dry assemble the bases by folding in the largest flap and then folding the two side flaps over it. Finally, slip the tongue flap into place to give a firm base. The tops of the boxes are designed so that the patterns interlink to hold them together with twining rosebuds or a pretty bow.

BASKET AND FRUIT PUNNET

Cut out the pages at the back of the book, then cut out the boxes using a cutting mat and knife or embroidery scissors. Make up the boxes using the same method as described for the small rosebuds and ribbons boxes, making sure that the initial folds on the fruit punnet are at a slant to give a tapering shape. Curve the top of the punnet over and interlink the fruits at the top to close. The sides of the picnic basket fold over at the top, sealing it with a gingham cloth, perhaps enclosing something for a summer birthday.

Above *The colourful basket and fruit punnet will appeal to all ages. The fruit punnet has a gift tag printed on it ready for you to complete.*

Left *These dainty rosebuds and ribbons boxes are closed by interlinking the pattern pieces at the top.*

GIFT CARRIER BAG

On page 68 there is a template for a small carrier bag. You can print the template directly onto wrapping paper in a photocopier, cutting the paper to either A4 or A3 size, and enlarging the template to whatever size you wish. Place the wrapping paper design uppermost in the photocopier paper tray. The template will then print directly onto your chosen paper.

To make up the carrier bag fold and glue down the flaps along the top to form a strong firm edge through which the carrying handles can be attached. Crease the four lines forming the bag corners, then lightly crease inwards the lines marked along the sides as these will form the side pleats in the carrier's interior. Glue the long side flap inside to form the bag's shape; then glue the base of the bag, folding in the short end flaps first. Punch holes as marked and attach cord, string or a ribbon of your choice to form the bag's handles.

BOX WITH LID

The templates below for a box with a lid can be photocopied or traced and used over and over again. The templates are small, but you can enlarge them to whatever size you wish on a photocopier, perhaps making a series of boxes in gradated sizes. Alternatively, trace out the box onto a paper of your choice; use a heavier paper for a more robust box or a light paper if the box will be used for something that weighs little.

The box and its lid are made up in the same way. Fold along all the flap lines, then fold in the side flaps to form an upright box shape. Apply glue to the four overlapping side flaps and stick them to the inside of the box. Secure the box by sticking down the narrower flaps over the top. Repeat for the lid.

Below *Templates for lidded box. It is easiest to paint decoration onto your box before gluing the pieces together.*

Opposite *Template for a gift carrier bag to make up in whatever decorative paper you wish.*

These stand-up photograph frames have a folded backrest. The lampshade matches the large frame and can be used with a bulb or candle light.

PHOTOGRAPH FRAMES

In the template section at the back of the book there are some photograph frames for you to cut out and use. They are easy to make and simply need to be folded to stand upright. Make up these frames to give as presents or use them yourself. If you prefer you could use the frames as templates for your own designs, tracing them out onto strong card and painting an appropriate decoration on them.

MAKING UP THE FRAMES

Cut out the template pages at the back of the book, then cut out the frames individually with a knife on a cutting mat or with a small pair of embroidery scissors. The frames can be used as they are or, if you require them to be a little more robust, glue the pages onto another piece of card, then cut the frames out by cutting through both layers at the same time for accuracy. Cut along the outlines of the frames' backrests, leaving the dotted lines intact.

Apply a little glue to the interior of each frame and glue your photo into position. Then pull out the frame's backrest and glue both the inner parts of the frame together, folding along the central dotted line, and thus enclosing the photo, with the backrest out. Use paperclips to hold the frame together while the glue dries, or clothes pegs if you are worried about marking the paper.

MATCHING LAMPSHADE

The cut-out lampshade at the back of the book matches the decoration on the front of the large photo frame at the back of the book. Again you could use this as a template by tracing off the shade onto strong card and applying your own decorative detail. I have also decorated the back of the frame to make it more interesting and this is another idea that you could take up if making a plain card lampshade, choosing your own theme.

The small lamp requires a metal holder, either the type that clips on over a bulb or a candle follower that is used with a straight-sided candle. If you want to use a candle remember not to leave it unattended when lit, just to be on the safe side. Glue the ends of the lampshade over one another, applying paperclips while the glue dries, and you will have a charming little shade to illuminate your photographs.

Below *The photograph frames and lampshade are easy to make – simply cut them out carefully and glue them.*

Pictures and photographs can often be enhanced by the the way they are mounted and it is tempting to experiment with the vast variety of papers now available. There are papers that have dried flowers trapped in the pulp, neat and snappy brightly coloured corrugated papers and textured watercolour papers. The choice of weights ranges from strong and thick utility coloured card to papers so fine that they would blow away in the slightest breeze. As well as using them for mounting pictures there are so many lovely papers to use for covering and binding albums and booklets or kitting out the kids wth attractive folders and files to go back to school.

SIMPLE MOUNTS AND BOOKBINDING

Opposite *An eye-catching series of prints colourfully mounted and framed.*

STEP BY STEP
*C*UTTING MOUNTING BOARD

Professional framers cut mounts with a deeper border at the bottom of the picture, since this gives a better visual balance. The size of mount is your choice, but look around and see what good framers are doing or research small art galleries for adventurous ideas. For instance, for very tiny pictures you might like a contrasting large mount; I have seen exotic stamps and black and white photographs mounted in this way.

1 Measure your picture or print accurately. With a print it is easy to judge the edge as there is a defined indented border. With a freehand picture, however, it is more difficult to decide how much empty space to have around the image. I have used an antique white board with a slight texture to complement my print.

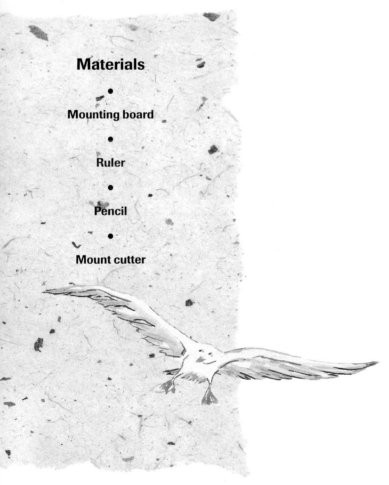

Materials

- **Mounting board**
- **Ruler**
- **Pencil**
- **Mount cutter**

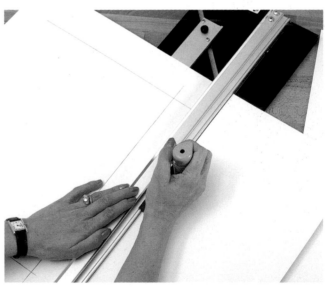

2 As this is a small print I allowed for a 6 cm (2 ⅜ in) border at the top and sides and 7 cm (2 ¾ in) along the bottom on the mount. Mark out the back of the mount with both the inner and outer measurements of the print. Slice the mount out of the board, pressing down firmly onto the guide ruler and drawing the blade towards you.

3 Again working from the back of your mount, line up the mounting board against the ruler guideline. Using a 45-degree bevel mount cutter, push the cutter into the mount board along your inner marked line to accommodate the print measurements. Holding the guide ruler firmly, push the bevel mount cutter away from you to the next marked corner. If you get it right the first time, well done; if not, it is exceptionally difficult to recut so unless the cut is really out do not try to correct it.

4 The best way to achieve a good alignment is to attach small strips of masking tape to the back of the print and lower the mounting board over the top. There are many variations to mounting work; you could make a slightly larger mount and double mount your picture, giving it greater emphasis. Use a ready-made frame with glass.

ℬATHING BEAUTIES

I found the amusing prints on page 72 at the Portobello market in London and their paper surrounds were badly damaged, so they had to be mounted. I chose a thick specialized mounting board to surround the prints. Mounting boards are available in a variety of textures, diverse grains and fabric finishes, and you can choose from over fifty colours, from the subtle to the bright.

MEASURING THE MOUNT

If you live in a remote area, many boards are available by mail order and usually travel well. The main decision to make when mounting your pictures is how large or small you want your surround to be. It is advisable when cutting any mount to give the measurement just 1 cm (½ in) more at the base as it helps the general proportions of the total framed area.

EXTENDING THE BACKGROUND

On cutting the mounts and placing them over the small prints, I found that the pictures lost some of their jovial atmosphere, so I decided to extend the sand a little onto the paper mount and draw the horizon in. Then I coloured in a little sea and became quite carried away and you see the result. I thoroughly enjoyed continuing the design on all the prints, tracing out a little boat from one print and painting it onto the surrounding mount of another. From a children's book on 'what we see at the sea' I included parasols, a lighthouse and a deck chair. With the closed interior of the changing rooms I used a ruler to continue the proportions from the main picture and added odd bits of clothing left about; my daughter's bedroom was inspiration for that! I love the cry of sea gulls and enjoyed including a rather fat one flying overhead.

OSTENDE.

Nᵒ 56.

All right !!

The seaside prints have been enhanced by further painted decoration on the mounts, extending the image and creating more dimension.

Testing your ideas

If you want to try an idea out before committing yourself to the whole mount, just cut a scrap piece of paper and make a false corner. Attach it lightly to your print and then step well back and judge the effect.

CLOWNING AROUND

These colourful clowns are still waiting to dance. They were saved for a rainy day over fifty years ago and thankfully never used. Now they can be photocopied and may dance many times over. I wanted the mounts to be simple as the prints are strong, so I picked out colours in the prints with surrounding coloured pencil lines.

Below *Plain white mounts have been decorated with simple coloured lines to emphasize the colours of the clowns and to coordinate with the frames.*

COLOURING THE FRAMES

There are many creative possibilities when decorating mounts. Pop your head into any good gallery and you will return home full of ideas. I coloured the plain wooden frames myself; it is always the least expensive solution. I used acrylic paints, which are available in a huge range of tempting colours. Apply each layer as the tiniest watered-down amount of paint possible and build up several layers of thin paint until you achieve the colour that you require. By putting your own ideas into practice you will accomplish positive and individual solutions to your framing needs.

A variety of stand-up photograph frames made from strong corrugated paper. Available in bright colours, this paper is ideal for the purpose.

CORRUGATED FRAMES

The natural strength of corrugated paper lends itself to framing. It is a light material and as the corrugations are attached to the flat cardboard beneath, the two layers are much easier to cut than a dense board. Returning from a family holiday in the snow I decided to frame small parts of our photographs together. These combination frames are excellent for those of us not gifted with the camera and enables you to select the area of the picture you like the best.

Lay out a large selection of your photographs and separately trace all the different apertures shown here; some of these overlap as we wanted to fit as many in as possible. Most of the apertures can be used horizontally or vertically. Place the tracings over your photographs to select which suits which best. I quite like to repeat the same aperture for sequence shots.

I have used a double frame; just one paper with a contrasting paper on top to give a better finish. Each aperture has a dotted inner line that is the first 'mount' paper; only a tiny border will show. The full line represents the paper that will front your frame. Trace the dotted frames out onto your underpaper, lining up any that are in sequence with a ruler, and cut them out using a cutting knife and mat. Paste your photographs into position with PVA glue, cutting away areas that are unnecessary or will not be seen.

Then line up the apertures, this time tracing out the full lines, and cut out the card. Place the front paper over the inner paper and glue into position. To give the multi-frame an additional border I laid contrasting green corrugated paper across the back in the opposite direction. If you are making many multi-frames for presents, it is worth making a complete tracing of all your apertures together to save a lot of time spent lining up later.

The smaller corrugated frames are a simple variation, with a folded paper prop to make them stand.

Choose the apertures you require and trace the shapes off separately. You can enlarge or reduce them in size by first photocopying and then tracing the outlines.

FOLDERS, BOOKLETS AND ENVELOPES

However many files are in the house there always seems one too few, especially when the children go back to school. It is important that files should look attractive; a new subject at school has a better chance of success in a snappy folder. A metal eyelet punch will give your work greater durability as well as look neater; punches are readily available at craft suppliers.

Brightly coloured beads decorate a range of files, folders and stationery items secured with elastic.

Primary colours for primary needs

The sheets of wonderful coloured card that are now available are excellent for making stationery items. For robust files or folders choose a 300 gsm (140 lb) weight; for lighter booklets a 140 gsm (65 lb) should be adequate; down to 90 gsm (40 lb) or 60 gsm (30 lb) for envelopes.

USING BEADS AND ELASTIC

The beaded document wallets shown here are easy to make. Round elastic allows for an expanding folder; the beads add a touch of decoration and if desperate could be used for counting! To construct your folder follow the pattern of one you already have. Use the eyelet punch in the same positions and thread your elastic through, securing each elastic end in a flat bead and looping the elastic over the corner of the folder to secure it.

Double elastic makes a practical binding for double papers to be bound into a folder. To keep the folder neatly closed, place metal eyelets on the back cover and attach elastic, so it can neatly hold the front cover, as in the red folder here. The small green folder demonstrates the use of elastic for a practical and decorative spine binding. The yellow booklet is an adaptation using two layers of paper; the top yellow layer has a small heart cut out and shows the green backing behind. Inside is a notepad held with elastic onto the back paper.

There are many variations that you can make using metal eyelets and elastic. The envelopes which I frequently use as packaging for presents are folded square with a small off-cut of card attached with a metal eyelet; I wind contrasting thread around behind the small card shape and then around the envelope to close it.

Albums made for special occasions or to record memories may one day become treasured heirlooms, so they deserve extra care in the making.

$\mathcal{N}$OSTALGIA ALBUMS

Albums that you create yourself are very personal. They can conserve memories of weddings – the guests, the menu, all those little forgotten details; they can record the precious first year of each new baby; they can remind you of voyages and holidays – with notes, maps, the names of people you meet and places you visit, good restaurants and meals; or they can catalogue your favourite collection.

CHOOSING PAPERS

The four albums here are made from stacks of larger sheets of paper cut down. The reason that I make them like this is that it is less expensive, it gives me a greater choice of papers and I like the look of torn edges.

Chose a thick 140 gsm (65 lb) paper for the outer cover; the rough-textured watercolour papers used here come in a selection of pastel shades. The bound pages are cut sheets of varying tones of the same type of paper. For one album I used shades of orange, yellow and cream, with an antique white cover, and bound it in string with bamboo. Another has a thick white cover and contains pages of subtle pinks and powdery blues bound with gold; the first and last papers are delicate tissue papers to add a little extra finesse; and the cover is decorated with small scraps of the tissue and golden writing on tracing paper. Etched flowers adorn the cover of an album made of stronger blue papers held in raffia over a straight twig. Older photographs held with traditional corners decorate another album bound with round black elastic wound over the spine; the pages in autumnal colours complement sepia and black and white photographs.

ALBUM SPINES

The spines of the albums here were each bound differently.

The bamboo has two holes bound down with double string. Thread the string from the back of the album over the bamboo and back through the same hole; take the thread along the back of the album over the bamboo and tie it on the album front. To avoid the string fraying, tie knots on the ends.

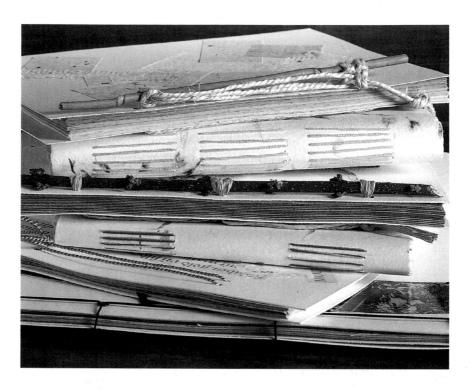

The thickly bound yellow threads accommodate a full booklet; double pages are attached by sewing with toning thread. Pierce through the sheets of paper with a hat pin.

The album decorated with a twig has three holes pierced along the edges of the cover. Thread the raffia from the back over the twig and back down the same hole; the raffia spans the back of the album to the middle hole, then threads through the paper over the twig and back down the same hole: repeat for the top hole. The raffia lies down the back of the album and ties off neatly with the starting end.

The orange booklet has double pages stitched into place, which makes an attractive spine when contrasting thread is used.

The golden-threaded album requires two sets of holes side by side at the top and bottom of the album. Again use a hat pin to pierce all the paper layers. If your cord is too thick for a needle, wind a small amount of tape into a point over the cord end

to stop it fraying and to act as a substitute needle. Thread the cord into one hole and out of the other, and repeat next to it, with the cord resting on the album's front. Then tie the cord attractively.

The photograph album bound in black elastic has been stitched through using a large needle. Begin 'sewing' from the bottom of the book; pierce four holes up the side using a hat pin to penetrate several layers of paper at once. With a very long elastic, begin sewing up the album through all the papers in large tacking stitches. On arrival at the top do one stitch around the spine and back into the same hole, then tack down to the second hole and do another large stitch around the spine, returning to the second hole. Continue along the spine and tie off any spare elastic at the bottom.

Above *Coloured threads, cords, twigs and raffia, tied or sewn, make secure and attractive bindings for hand-made notebooks and albums.*

GARDENING NOTES

Part of the pleasure of making your own booklets is choosing the paper to suit your needs. Dried-flower paper is expensive, but is a wonderful treat for the cover of this booklet. I like to combine papers within the booklet, with watercolour paper for a painting here and there, and writing paper for notes on when the flower was planted, the soil used and the flower's individual needs.

MEASURING PAGES

First choose your booklet cover, which should be of at least 140 gsm (65 lb) weight paper; all the paper pages can be of varying weights. Measure out the pages to be 1 cm (½ in) smaller than the cover, and allow for the paper to be folded in half to make double pages. Depending on the weight of your paper you will be able to double up a 90 gsm (40 lb) paper with 60 gsm (30 lb) or put three 60 gsm (30 lb) papers together and stitch them in double or triple thickness.

SEWING DOUBLE PAGES

Then with coloured embroidery threads and a large needle sew through the open fold of the interior papers through the booklet cover and back to the open double page, back out to the booklet cover and back into the double paper again. Firmly anchor your paper into place by tying a knot at each end for security. As you insert more paper and sew it in double pages you will build up a thick spine.

MARBLED-PAPER NOTEBOOKS

The colours in marbled papers are quite sumptuous, with unpredictable and unique patterns. These hand-made papers weigh only 90 gsm (40 lb) or 150 gsm (70 lb) so you need to back them with another paper for greater

durability. I have folded a lot of paper within the notebooks to make them bulky in order to use them for a long time. The papers are sewn into the cover with toning threads, making attractive books to use for all sorts of purposes.

Many craft and specialist paper shops sell hand-made papers, and no two marbled papers are exactly alike.

This gardening notebook, with a dried-flower paper cover, has watercolour pages interleaved for sketches and paintings.

*Origami is the Japanese art of paper folding; many varied forms can be
created by folding a square of paper and following a pattern. As a child I had
a Japanese friend and we sat for hours folding long interlinking origami
paper-chain garlands, made with beautifully toning papers that subtly
changed in colour as each origami link of the garland progressed. She wore
them around her neck with a traditional kimono at her tenth birthday party
and gave each of her small guests a strand to take home; I kept mine for years.
All the scraps of paper that you might have accumulated from making other
projects could be saved and used for origami.*

ORIGAMI

Opposite *Christmas tree decorated with origami
Santa Clauses and stars, and wrapped presents underneath.*

STEP BY STEP
ƒANTA CLAUS

A number of Santa Clauses decorate the Christmas tree on page 86, but they could also be used for labels or sent as original Christmas cards with a message written on the back. You can make a small, fat Santa Claus by sinking the body well into the legs or a long, thin Santa Claus by only gluing the body and legs together at the tips of the paper. The choice is yours; each Santa Claus will have his own character.

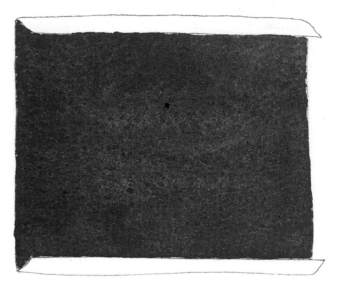

1 Take one square of paper. With the red side facing you, fold over the top and bottom to form two small cuffs.

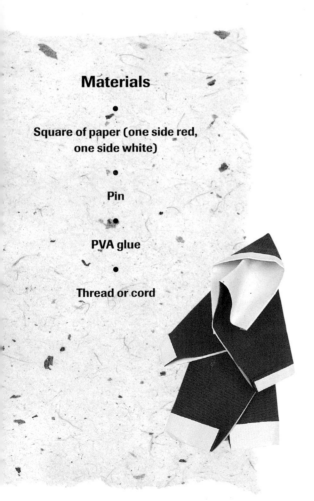

Materials

• Square of paper (one side red, one side white)

• Pin

• PVA glue

• Thread or cord

2 Place a pin prick, which will be seen both sides, one third of the way down the paper in the middle. With the white side facing you, fold across the pin prick, the top left-hand corner across the paper to halfway down the right side. Press the fold into the paper.

3 Again using the pin prick as a marker, fold the right side over on top of the left, forming Santa Claus's two arms. Press firmly on the fold.

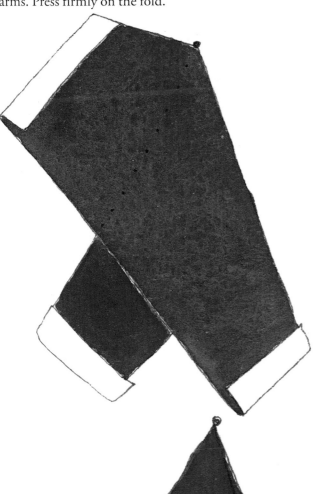

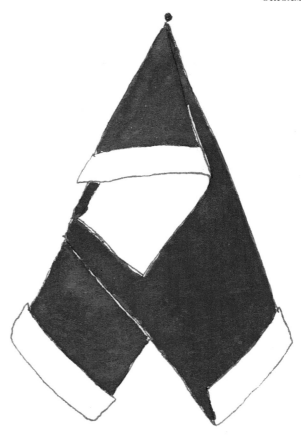

4 To create Santa Claus's head fold the extended piece of paper back flat onto itself. This forms Santa Claus's hood with projected face extended. Press firmly around Santa Claus's hood

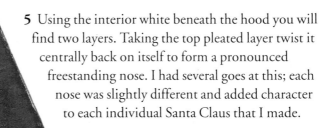

5 Using the interior white beneath the hood you will find two layers. Taking the top pleated layer twist it centrally back on itself to form a pronounced freestanding nose. I had several goes at this; each nose was slightly different and added character to each individual Santa Claus that I made.

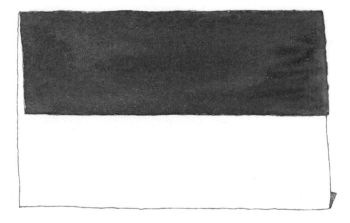

6 To fold Santa Claus's legs another paper is needed. Fold the paper a third of the way over, red onto white, and turn back a small white cuff behind at the bottom for his trousers.

7 Fold the right side of the paper to form a leg with small trouser cuff to a little over half the paper. Smooth down the side of the trouser leg crease.

8 Fold the left-hand side over the right 'leg' to give Santa Claus two legs with small cuffs. Do not worry if the legs differ slightly; it will look as if Santa Claus is tripping along when you make him up. Turn under any excess paper that is protruding over his leg and generally tidy him up.

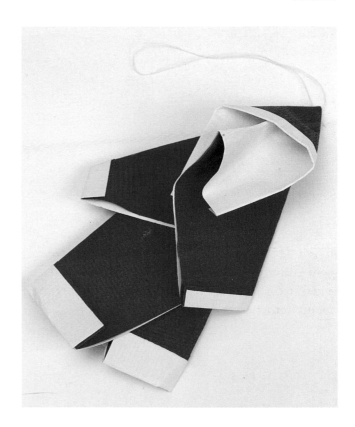

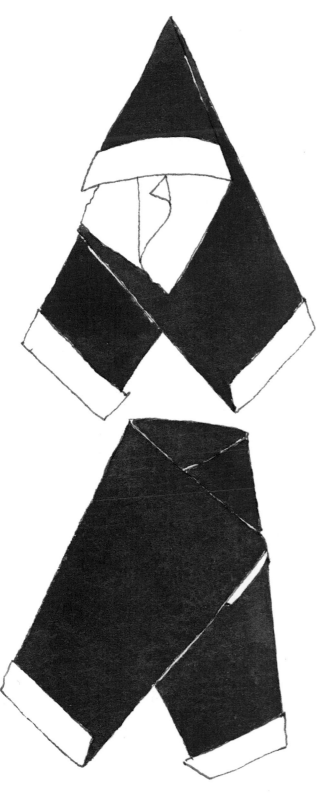

9 Place the body of Santa Claus over his legs. Different legs and different bodies all give Santa Claus a different gait. If you are going to hang him up glue the two pieces together and add a thread to the top of his hood.

The front and back of the finished Santa Claus, with cord attached for hanging on the Christmas tree.

STEP BY STEP
$\mathcal{L}$UCKY STAR

I learnt how to make these stars by watching a Chinese girl ripping lengths of her sketchbook and idly making 'lucky stars', as she called them. Each star is made just by tying a knot in a long strip of paper. Nothing could be simpler, and they are so pretty, so do have a go! They can be used to decorate the Christmas tree or as a decoration on presents as shown on page 86.

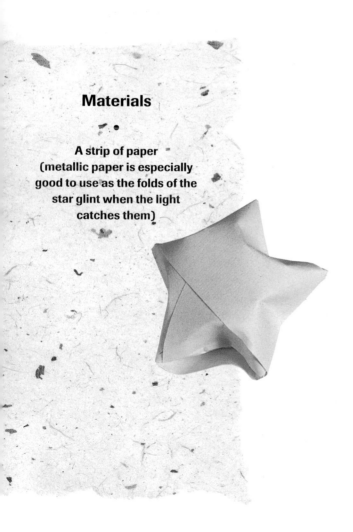

Materials

A strip of paper (metallic paper is especially good to use as the folds of the star glint when the light catches them)

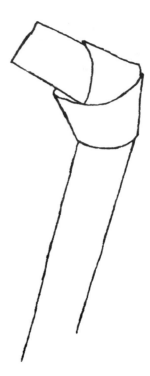

1 Just tie a knot into the end of a strip of paper. Take one end, left over right, behind and up through the loop, and pull through to the left.

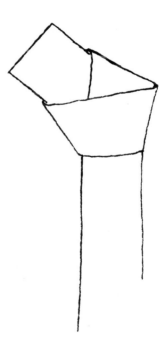

2 Then flatten out the knot and you will have created a perfect pentagon shape with five sides and equal angles.

3 Tuck the loose knot end into the centre.

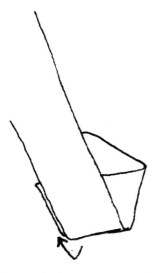

4 Fold the tail over the knot pentagon form.

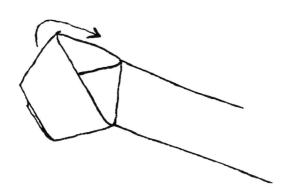

5 Fold the tail behind the knot pentagon form. Each time the paper will naturally lie along the pentagon edge. Repeat until the pentagon star has been covered once to form a double paper layer.

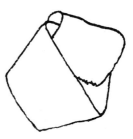

6 Tuck in the loose end of paper underneath the pentagon star shape fold.

7 Push in the sides to form a three-dimensional star; complete all sides. Some stars are determined not to push in perfectly and need a helpful long needle poked inside to push them out; others work first time.

8 The completed star. Attach a thread or cord if you wish to use the star as a hanging decoration.

Wishing on a star

You can make bowls full of these stars, writing messages inside for good will, or perhaps romantically send them to someone special.

PLEATED PRESENTS WRAPPING

The natural elegance of pleated plain paper is a wonderful treat.
I remember as a child watching my mother pleating presents for
my grandmother and being intrigued by the whole process.

*Plain wrapping paper takes
on a special quality when
neatly pleated. An origami
'lucky star' containing a
message completes the gift.*

DRAMATIC GIFTS

The simplest way to pleat paper is
to have two folds going at right
angles against each other, as with
the black present, which was a
book, shown under the Christmas
tree on page 86. The larger flat
white present (also a book!) has
diagonal pleats running across a
corner, and so does the black small
box present tucked beneath the tree.

I particularly like to combine
two colours of paper, a technique
that often shows the pleated paper
to the greatest advantage. The
smaller white present has a section
of black pleating running over one
end. The largest present is first
covered with a layer of black paper.
The white paper is then laid over
the black, but instead of wrapping
it over it is folded back diagonally
across the present and then pleated
back on itself.

Try experimenting with the
differing colours on each side of
your paper. In Europe wrapping
paper normally has a pattern on
one side, while the reverse side is
plain. In the USA, however, paper
is available with differing patterns
on each side; I find this paper
delightful for different wrapping
effects. Recipients of presents are
often as taken with the wrapping
as with the gift inside.

SUPPLIERS

**Daler-Rowney Fine Art
and Graphic Materials,**
Daler-Rowney House,
Bracknell, Berkshire RG12 8ST.
Tel 01344 424621.
Fax 013344 486511.
Working with these exceptionally
high quality products always gives
the best results. The papers are
versatile and sumptuous, the
brushes hard wearing and subtle.
I use many of the products available,
from the lightest tissue paper to
thickest paint. A full 128-page
catalogue demonstrates the diversity
of the products and gives
constructive use of materials.

Quart de Poil at The Holding
Company, 243-245 Kings Road,
London SW3.
Olivier Leblois designed the
charming child's desk and chair
on page 62. A similar design is
also available for adults, along
with many other pieces of
cardboard furniture. Liaison
and distribution office:
83 Harestone Hill, Caterham,
Surrey CR3 6DL.
Tel/Fax 01883 343242.

Creative Kids Company Ltd,
Swansea SA6 8RB.
Tel 01792 790726.
Fax 01792 781075.
Suppliers of instant papier mâché,
sold in dry powder form to which
water is added; very easy and saves a
lot of work making your own.

Price's Patent Candles,
110 York Road, Battersea,
London SW11 3RU.
Tel 0171 228 3345.
Fax 0171 738 0197.
An exceptional range of straight-
sided candles plus candle followers
ideal for the lampshade projects in
the book.

V. V. Rouleaux,
10 Symons Street,
Sloane Square,
London SW3 2TJ.
Tel 0171 730 3125.
Fax 0171 730 3468.
An exceptional selection of ribbons,
braids, tassels and other trimmings,
also available via their comprehensive
mail order service.

Manuel Canovas,
2 North Terrace,
London SW3 2BA.
Tel 0171 225 2298.
Fax 0171 823 7848.
Beautifully designed fabrics.

$\mathscr{R}$EADY-TO-USE DESIGN TEMPLATES

The following templates are ready for you to cut out and use.
Alternatively, you could trace or photocopy them to enlarge or
reduce them, and add your own design.

FLOWER AND BUD STENCIL (see instructions pages 40–41)

SILHOUETTE BORDERS (see instructions pages 54–55)

LAMPSHADE (see instructions page 71)

LARGE PHOTOGRAPH FRAME (see instructions page 71)

SMALL PHOTOGRAPH FRAMES (see instructions page 71)

ROSES GIFT BOX (see instructions page 67)

RIBBONS GIFT BOX (see instructions page 67)

BASKET GIFT BOX (see instructions page 67)

FRUIT PUNNET GIFT BOX (see instructions page 67)

FLOWER AND BUD STENCIL

SILHOUETTE BORDERS

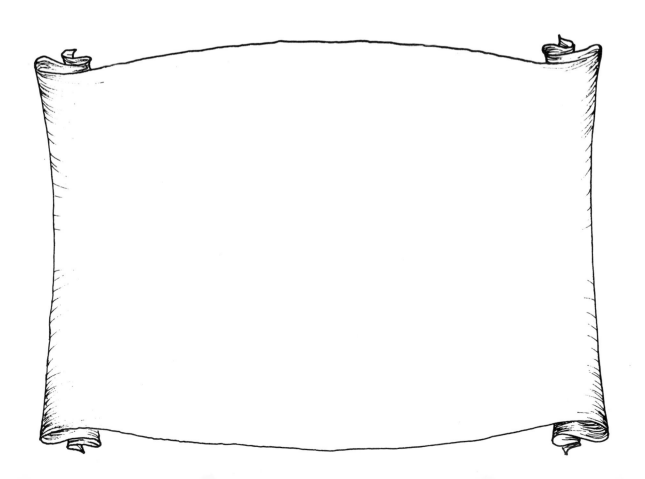

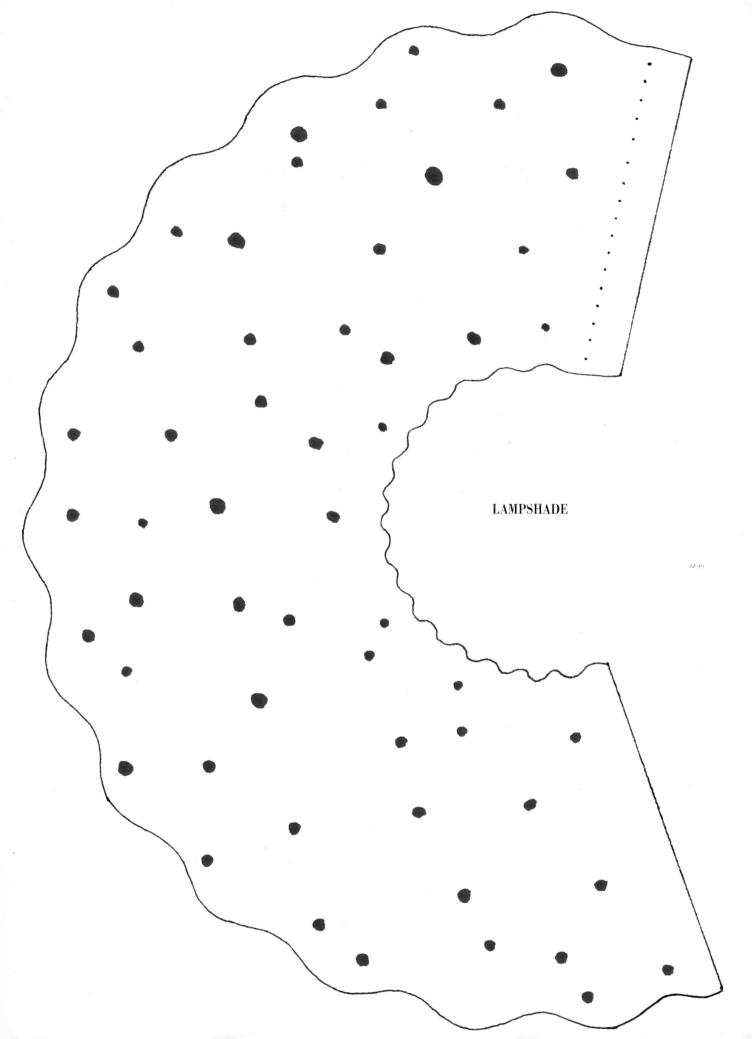

LAMPSHADE

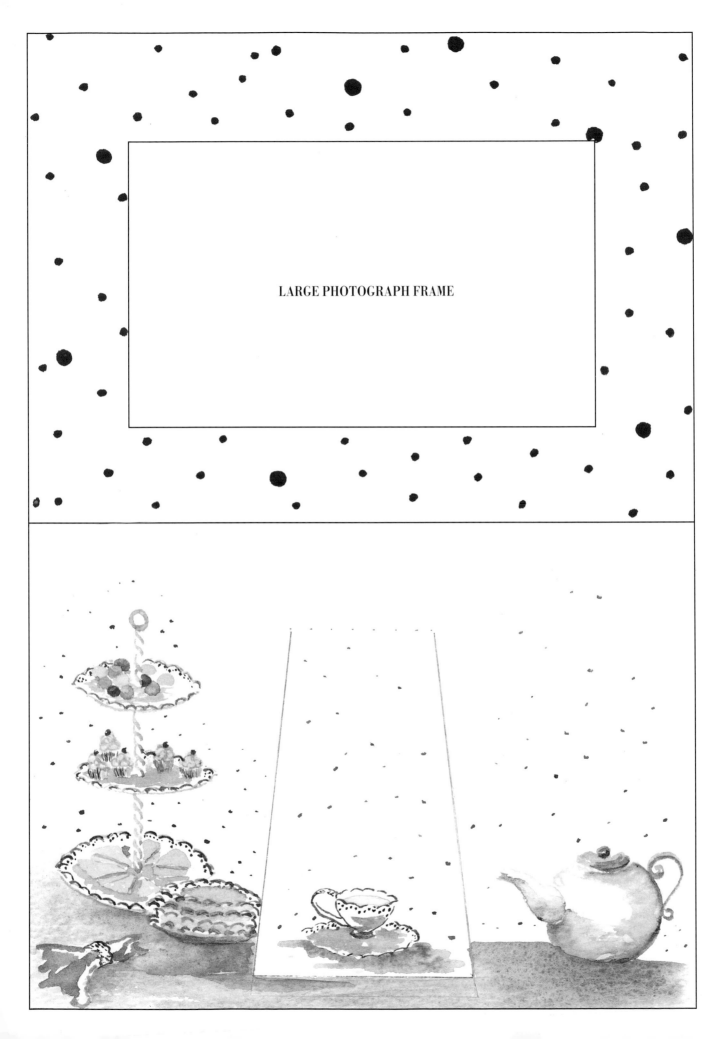

LARGE PHOTOGRAPH FRAME

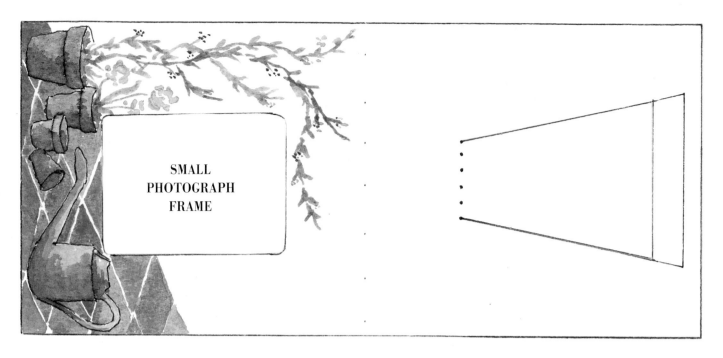

SMALL
PHOTOGRAPH
FRAME

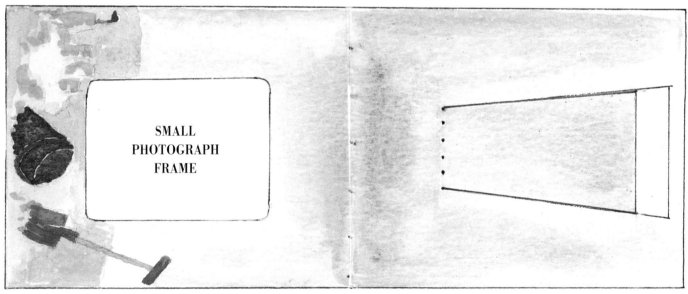

SMALL
PHOTOGRAPH
FRAME

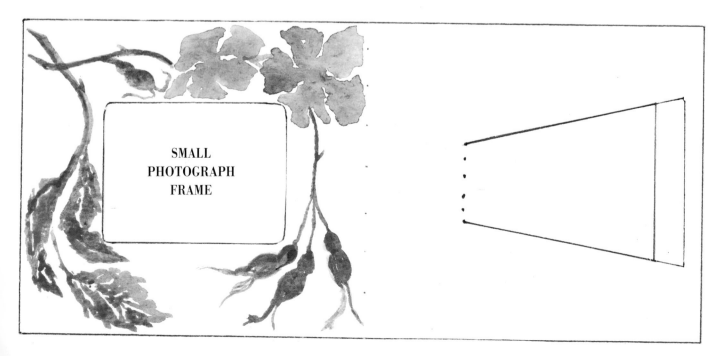

SMALL
PHOTOGRAPH
FRAME

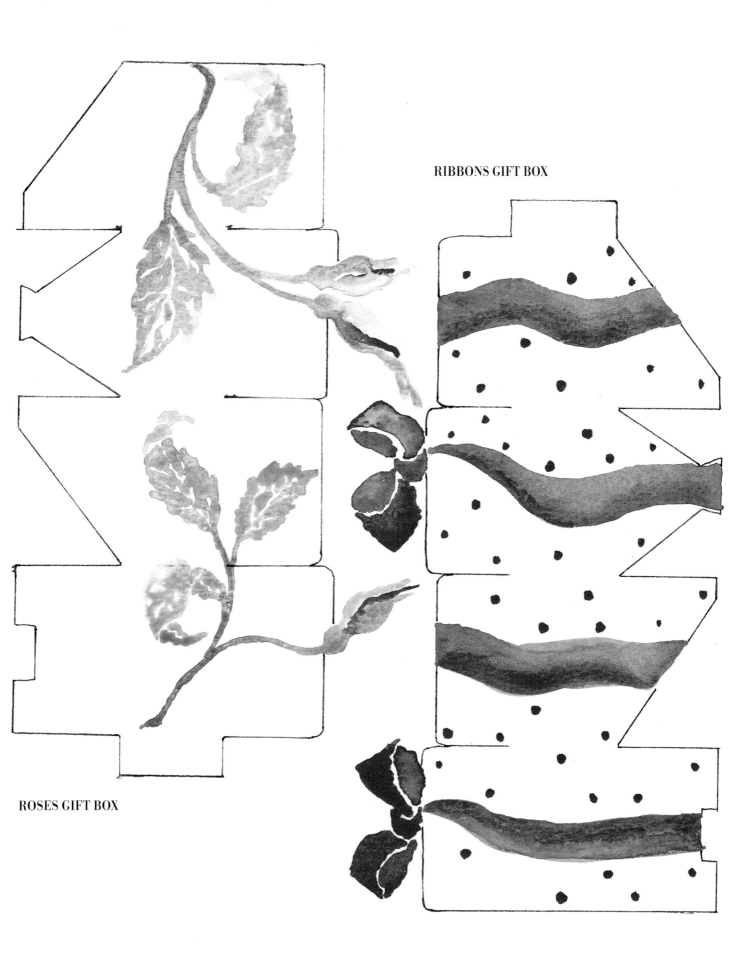

RIBBONS GIFT BOX

ROSES GIFT BOX

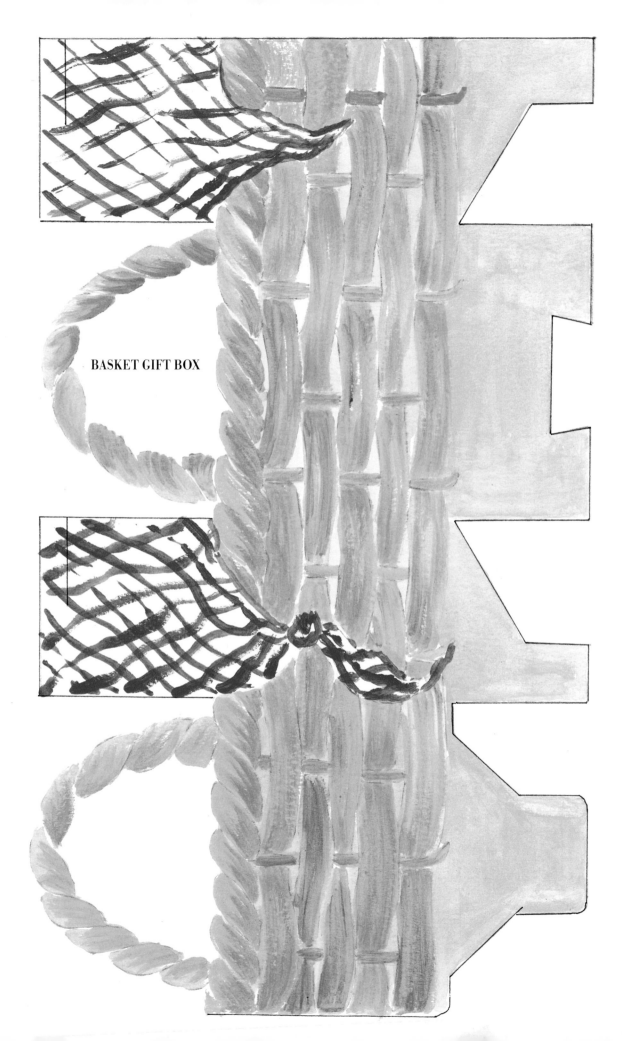

BASKET GIFT BOX

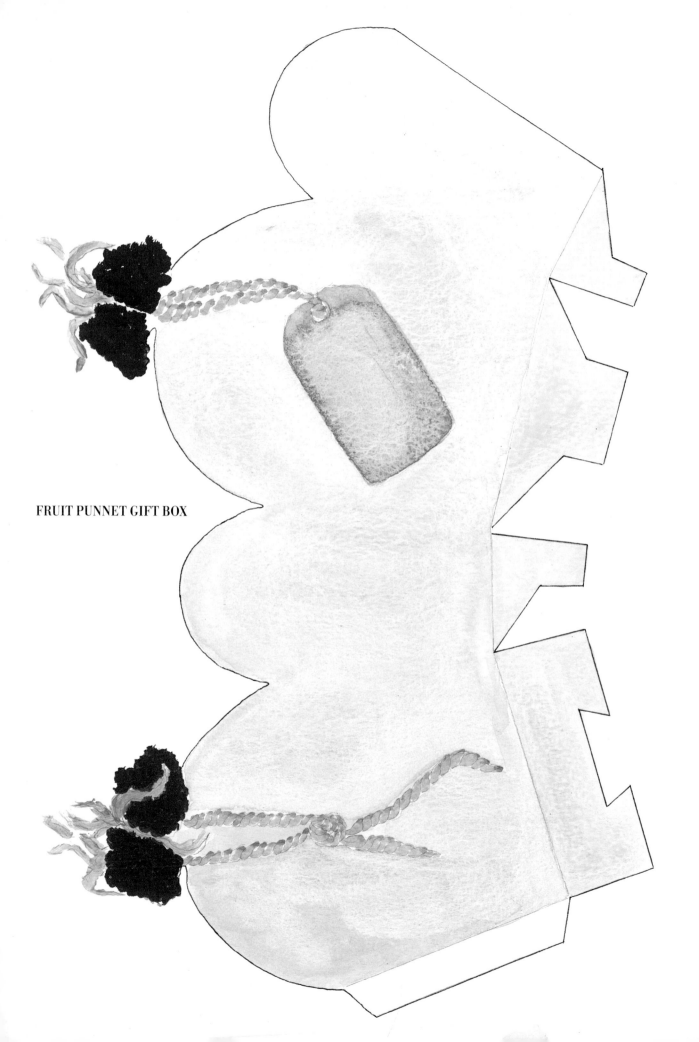

FRUIT PUNNET GIFT BOX